Moonraker County

A Wiltshire Guide

Moonraker County

A Wiltshire Guide

Lornie Leete-Hodge

ALAN SUTTON
1982

Alan Sutton Publishing Limited
17a Brunswick Road
Gloucester

First published 1982

British Library Cataloguing in Publication Data

Leete-Hodge, Lornie
    Moonraker county: Wiltshire guide.
    1. Wiltshire (England) — Description and travel
    I Title
    914.23'104858   DA670.W7

    ISBN 0-904387-92-5

Typesetting and origination by
Alan Sutton Publishing Limited.
Photoset Baskerville 11/12.
Printed in Great Britain
by Page Bros (Norwich) Limited

For Millicent Leete

This book is dedicated to the memory of the First Freeman of the Borough of Devizes.

Contents

Introduction

'Know this thy countie, Wiltshire, look up and thank God.' These words headed the programme for an Annual Dinner of Wiltshiremen in London, some forty years ago, yet, to a true Moonraker, like myself, who loves their heritage, they are worthy and meaningful today.

Wiltshire – never referred to by those who know as 'Wilts' – is a strange, compelling county, populated by men and women who possess a rugged independence and a long acquired ability to come to terms with life. Those who dismiss us as rustics – and there have been many over the years – have learned a hard lesson. Not many can equal a Wiltshireman on his own territory or match his natural born cunning. Their nickname – Moonrakers – used in a derisive manner in the last century, proved those very men were fully alert.

For those who do not know the legend here is the story. Some Wiltshire smugglers were carrying illicit brandy when they were surprised by the Excisemen. Quickly, they pushed the barrels into a pond and began raking with long rakes. Laughing, the Excisemen wanted to know what they were doing. "Raking up the cheese," replied the Moonrakers, pointing to the moon's reflection in the water, and amused (and taken in) at their imagined stupidity, the Excisemen went their way, leaving the Moonrakers to fish out their brandy in peace. They had the last laugh!

Some find their dry humour hard to understand. They are proud of their county, their heritage, and have a take it or leave it attitude to those "furriners" who visit them. I have often heard it said that Wiltshiremen are glad there is no sea to attract all the visitors one watches in a lemming-stream, racing across the county at weekends in pursuit of pleasure.

Moonrakers possess the cunning of a fox. They lean over their gates and watch the world go by, for in a county as old as Wiltshire, they can truthfully say they have seen it all before. They know they will endure when the tempests and troubles have passed, and, since Roman times when the great Legions poured across the Plain and tried to make roads, the locals watched and waited. They knew the grass would grow again and all trace of the invaders removed. It was the same in the last War. The military came in droves and set up their camps. One such untidy straggle of huts and impedimenta on the Salisbury Road, fell into ruin when the "captains and kings departed" and nature claimed back her own land. Now sheep wander free once more and all trace of the "invasion" has long been healed by time.

For centuries, men have come and tried to conquer Wiltshire, but, somehow, maybe secretly laughing the while, the county has defeated them. The timeless past is ever present, and it is a county of the unexpected — one can drive for miles across the wide, beautiful emptiness of the Plain, or down a valley, turn a corner and see an old mill house with dappling millrace happily plashing in crescent foam to the river. Or pause on a stretch of lonely downland and listen to the sound of larks on the still air, for it was not for nothing that one place is called Larkhill, where the sweet song still triumphs over the noise and bustle of the army who disturbed their peace.

On an outline map, Wiltshire closely resembles the squat profile of a primitive man — the edges touch the boundaries of Berkshire, Hampshire, Somerset, Avon, Gloucestershire and Dorset with no seas bordering any of its borders. It appears to some as an island pasture whose landscape is an ocean of rolling grass encompassing Salisbury Plain which has a matchless quality all its own. The county holds a fascination for its children – though they will not always admit it – seeming to breed in them a doggedness and tenacity of purpose born of the wide, wild terrain and the tranquillity of the open downs. They fear no one, they are sufficient in themselves and long, long ago when it was a densely populated wooded area, they learned to come to terms with its reality.

The main feature of the county is, of course, the great three hundred square miles of Salisbury Plain, for centuries the training ground for soldiers. Across the downs which are the root and origin of the history of Wiltshire, are tracks as old as the monoliths and barrows with which they abound.

Some, ignorant of the real charm of Wiltshire, think the great stretches of its downs – its greatest strength – rude and bare, but, therein, for many, lies its beauty. The clear, untrammelled distances, the vast expanse of open grassland that forms Salisbury Plain is match-less. For centuries, the army has found it excellent as a training ground and, driving across the Plain today, one can still see the warning red flags or tanks moving across its space. In the last War, the whole Wiltshire village of Imber on the Down was commandeered by the military for training purposes and its inhabitants evacuated. It proved its worth and has never been returned to its people, though they are allowed to make an annual pilgrimage to the Church in the summer.

Little can match the magnificence and majesty of Stonehenge, set in the heart of the Plain since time immemorial. It is perhaps typical of Wiltshiremen that this great mystery which has remained unsolved for thousands of years, puzzling the keenest brains of every age, is "just part of the scenery" to them, accepted and used to advantage where possible.

There are those who think those other stones, the Great Circle, at Avebury, more inspiring, and there is a feeling about both places that is unique, a timelessness and sense of awe and wonder that makes present-day living a triviality. To stand and look at Stonehenge or Avebury in the coming twilight on a summer's evening, with the lengthening shadows flickering on the stones, is an experience to enhance the life of any thinking person.

Evidence of the unique attraction of the downs is proved by this tale of an exile – an unknown man – who years ago lay dying alone in London. Asked if there was anything he wanted, he replied, "The Marlborough Downs". Maybe he felt he would draw strength from

The downs of Salisbury Plain which are the root and origin of the history of Wiltshire,

Avebury, the village of the stones, holds more than a hint of mystery.

their beauty. The Marlborough Downs – the stretch from Devizes to Marlborough in particular possess a wonderful sense of majesty, especially when an approaching storm darkens the hills and the whole appears a brooding giant. Then a shaft of sunlight touches the tips and the panorama of beauty is unsurpassed.

For its size, Wiltshire is one of the most thinly populated counties in England, with only three towns with a population over twelve thousand. The quality of continuity is inherent, and, for generations, the same families have lived in the same villages. In Wilton, in particular, once the proud capital of Wessex which gave its name to the county, names are still found in the twentieth century which were first recorded in 1544.

Their inheritance is magnificent – the three mightiest prehistoric

12

monuments in England – probably in Europe – one of the most beautiful Cathedrals and a lush, green forest that is unique – apart from the towns and villages which have their own stories to relate.

Wiltshire has much natural beauty, including its rivers. The Wylye, beloved of fishermen, the Nadder and the Ebble with villages along their banks, and the Kennet in the north and Avon to the west. The Kennet and Avon Canal which decimates the centre of the county was an engineering feat in its day and much used for transport, though the coming of the railways brought its decline, and it is used for pleasure today.

At Chilmark in the Nadder Valley are the famous stone quarries from which many of the great buildings, including the Cathedral, have been made since medieval times.

The county developed naturally as a general progression – the farmers in the north favoured dairying, with sheep on the Plain in the south. The county was, for the most part, untouched by medieval wars, and the villages and little townships grew and prospered, each very independent, particularly with the coming of the wool and weaving industries. Yet the county was still rural, indifferent to city life, a favourite haunt of kings and queens through the centuries. They loved to hunt in its forests (Henry VIII found his third wife in Savernake Forest) and Elizabeth I came to watch the building of Wilton and Longleat.

For many, the focal point of the county is Salisbury with its ever beckoning Cathedral spire dominating the skyline, and immortalised by Constable who often painted it.

There is much for the tourist to see – the great Cathedral in its fair city – Stonehenge, Avebury, Silbury, the White Horses cut into the chalk hillsides, Amesbury of legend, Wilton and the villages nestling in the river valleys, all seemingly looking towards the city.

There are many ancestral homes – Longleat, home of the Marquis of Bath, who was a pioneer in creating the first Safari Park of its kind in the county to share his home with thousands; Stourhead with its magnificent gardens designed by Capability Brown and known to those who saw it featured in the television version of *The Pallisers*. And some claim Wilton is the loveliest of them all. There are many more to see and enjoy.

The towns, too, claim a visit – Devizes, in the centre of the county and rich in its history, its market place used in *Far From the Madding Crowd* film; Marlborough, known for its great Public School has many features, its broad street and the legend of Merlin lingers still on the Castle and nearby Silbury Hill. Corsham, Calne, Chippenham all with their own attractions, and Bradford-on-Avon, once called "a melody of stone" – the list is endless.

Bradford-on-Avon, a town of antiquity nestling on the slopes all around it.

The traveller journeys on, often over the great coaching roads of the past still retaining their ancient hostelries – to Swindon with its bustling energy. Once a small market town, it grew with the coming of the railways. There is Castle Combe, another lovely village, the background for the film *Dr Dolittle* and little Aldbourne, the classic village of duckpond and village green used in *Dr Who* episodes, not forgetting the unchanging beauty of Lacock which is as medieval today as ever.

Wiltshire is proud of its heritage. It can offer history, indeed, prehistory, with its unsolved mysteries, fine properties owned by the National Trust and private owners, gentle rivers, magnificent downland which defies description, Moonrakers with a dry humour – where else would something like this true story happen? Siegfried Sassoon who lived and wrote in the soft south, drove into a pond one foggy night. Nothing was said to him, but the next day the owners put up a notice, THIS POND IS PRIVATE.

The County, for its size, has been a pioneer in many fields, bred many fine sons and daughters – it was the first county to raise its own

14

Police force in 1839, a Cavalry Regiment earlier, Sir Christopher Wren, Addison, the first Speaker of the House of Commons are among its legion children, all of whom are inevitably woven into the fabric of its life, making it one that will endure.

The Moonrakers possess an independence that is rare. They do not ask or expect a visitor to like Wiltshire – whether they do so and come to love its ruggedness like true natives, or they are forgotten as wisps of hay blown on a summer breeze. There is no compromise. To be accepted by the county is rare honour indeed, and I am proud that my father, a Scot, who came to Wiltshire some fifty years ago to devote his life to local government, was rewarded by the burgesses of Devizes who realised his qualities and afforded him their highest accolade. He became the then Borough's First Freeman in 1956, and no man could have been happier or more conscious of the honour conferred on him. It was his finest hour.

Time's hand has brought changes which are inevitable, and, like their ancestors, Moonrakers have accepted, though not always welcomed them. Roads and motorways bring the cities nearer and the farmer's role is different. Little communities are widening their spectrum, but with caution, and great care is taken to preserve the greatness of the past heritage.

My county is one to visit and to enjoy. Anyone taking time to pause and seek will be well rewarded for the harvest is a rich one, but, word of warning, do not expect to be accepted for the first twenty years. You will be welcomed for what you are, "a furriner", and you, like many others, will want to stay and become part of its life.

Wiltshire, to me, is wonderful with the quality of tenacity and tranquillity that has stood and passed the test of time.

1

Salisbury and the Plain

The story of this lovely city begins at Old Sarum, two miles north of
Salisbury. An Iron Age earthwork, it later became a Roman fort, and
the highest point is about four hundred feet above sea level with the
ramparts enclosing an area of some twenty-nine acres. It has the
appearance of an isolated hill, and is seen at its most magnificent on the
old Devizes road, a view John Constable liked to paint.

In Saxon times, it was an important political centre, a Witenagemot
being held there in 960. In 1070, William the Conqueror reviewed his
troops there and it became a bishopric with a Cathedral and Castle.

The first Cathedral was largely destroyed by a storm within days of
its consecration, only the nave surviving to be incorporated into Bishop
Roger's restoration. Osmund, a powerful Bishop and Chancellor of
England, finally completed the re-building of the damaged Cathedral
and established the Constitution based on the Chapter of the Bayeux
Cathedral in France. He also introduced a new order of Service known
as the Use of Sarum, on which much of our present day worship is still
based. He was canonised in 1457.

However, in 1220, the authorities decided to abandon the site after
problems had arisen between the military and the clergy. The old
Cathedral fell into ruin, many of its stones being used for the new
Cathedral at Salisbury. The town of Old Sarum declined and was
acquired by the Pitt family in 1705. In 1734, William Pitt, the Elder,
sat as Member of Parliament for Old Sarum and the hill was
represented in Parliament until 1852.

Two Sarsen commemorative stones near Old Sarum are of interest.
One marks the site of the old Parliamentary tree, cut down in 1905,
under which Old Sarum's MPs were elected up to 1831. The second at
the side of the main road marks the site at which Army measurements
were taken in the eighteenth century and formed the basis of Ordnance

In 1794
a line from this site
to Beacon Hill was measured by
Capt W Mudge of the Ordnance Survey,
as a base for the triangulation of,
Great Britain

Presented by Master Masons 1967

Old Sarum where the story of Salisbury began on this isolated hill, most magnificent from the Devizes road.

Survey maps. The first stone was, incidentally, cut by Ben Lloyd, a stonemason from Great Bedwyn.

The ruins of this site, showing the castle and two Cathedrals are well worth seeing, and the views of the surrounding area are outstanding.

Stratford-sub-Castle, lying in the hollows of Old Sarum, is another of the small, ancient camps that scatter Wiltshire.

The church was much enriched by the Pitt family, particularly Thomas Pitt, who became an East India merchant, and was known as 'Diamond' Pitt because of a diamond he purchased. It is now one of France's national jewels. The family home is now the Vicarage and chiefly remembered as the birthplace of William Pitt, the Earl of Chatham, grandson of Diamond Pitt.

There are still members of the Pitt family living in the village to this day.

And so on to Salisbury, the capital of the county and one of England's most attractive and outstanding cities with a rich and fascinating history woven into the tapestry of its development.

It was built in a chequered pattern on the confluence of four rivers and water channels once ran along every street. The inhabitants likened it to Venice, and someone's epitath read that he was born 'in the English Venice and died in the Italian'.

Most of the channels were filled in after the cholera epidemic in 1849, though the rivers still flow gently.

As may be expected, the Cathedral dominates the city, and, indeed, the surrounding area for the tall spire, rising some 404 feet into the sky can be seen for miles around. The foundations were laid in 1220 and many legends grew from the choice of site. Some say that the flight of an arrow shot by an archer from the ramparts of Old Sarum marked the place, another that the Virgin Mary appeared to Bishop Poore in a dream telling him to build on 'Mary's Field' which was the site selected, even though it was a low lying, marshy place.

The builder was a man from Norfolk, but the stone came from Chilmark quarries a few miles from the city. It was said it was built on wool sacks, and there was much doubt as to the wisdom of building on wet ground, but the builders were no fools and the evidence of their efforts is still magnificent today.

It is one of the few Cathedrals in the shape of a double cross with the arms of the transept branching off on either side, and is one of the larger of the English cathedrals, with the cloisters certainly bigger and older than any others. The spire, added a hundred years after the Cathedral was consecrated in the presence of Henry III in 1258, was the work of Richard Farley, a Wiltshireman whose remarkable achievement was the crowning glory to the edifice. The immense weight of the spire, of some six thousand tons meant much strengthening, but it has endured, though Sir Christopher Wren was asked to examine it and others since. As the Cathedral is a secular, not monastic one, the cloisters were not really necessary and are entirely isolated from the Cathedral.

The setting is perfect — the Cathedral is in one of the most attractive Closes in England, harmonising with the medley of houses that surround its walls. In 1327, Edward III gave permission for a wall to be erected surrounding the Cathedral, with gates, which still stand today and are locked each night.

More about the Close later, but, first, the interior of the Cathedral which has many unique treasures and much to see and enjoy. One of the most interesting is the ancient clock mechanism, dating from 1386,

In a perfect setting, Salisbury Cathedral harmonises amid a medley of houses in the Close.

and said to be the oldest piece of machinery still at work in Britain, possibly even in the world.

Naturally, there are many monuments to the Bishops — including two brasses — one of Bishop Wyvile, dated 1375, which is seven feet six inches long and unique in composition, for it shows the Bishop in his Castle of Sherborne with his champion beneath, and Bishop Geste is also commemorated, and there are many others.

The tomb of William Longespee Earl of Salisbury and half brother to King John is here — he witnessed the sealing of the Magna Carta, and there is an original copy brought from Runnymede in June 1215 by the Earl who gave it to the Cathedral for safekeeping.

Long years ago, the shrine of St Osmund was the scene of pilgrimage when many came to be cured of their ills. The Audley Chantry, a tiny chapel at the east end, was said to have been used as a blacksmith's shop by Cromwell's Roundheads during the Civil War, but, mercifully, they did not sack the building.

The monuments, rich and simple, are very varied. In one chapel to a courtier and maid of honour to Elizabeth I, is a window dedicated to George Herbert, the poet Vicar of Bemerton, whose poems were said to give peace and comfort to Charles I in his last days, and now they have been set to music are sung with pleasure as hymns in many churches. He was a simple, humble man, who died of consumption while still young, and he walked daily to the Cathedral for services. There is a fine tomb to Sir Richard Colt Hoare of Stourhead; the tomb of Sir Richard Mompesson (whose house lies in the Close); Lord Radnor with his Garter banner; Sir John Cheney who fought at Bosworth Field; James Harris (of Malmesbury House in the Close); Philip Sidney's sister, the Countess of Pembroke, Bishops, clergy and many many more. There is also the chantry of Walter Hungerford whose great family stretched its name across the county, holding manors and giving service to their nation. One of the family, (who originally came over the border from Somerset), was the first man entitled Speaker of the House of Commons.

Much of the old stained glass was destroyed in the eighteenth century, though some remains. It has been claimed that no building is more lucid, more logical or restful to the sight and mind. Originally, it was built with twelve doors in it, three hundred and sixty-five windows, and eight thousand columns holding it up — that is to say, a door for every month in the year, a window for every day and a column for every hour!

The Library contains the Sarum Breviary of 1440 and the Sarum Psalter amongst its many volumes and is open to view.

One of the greatest attributes of this great Cathedral is, undoubtedly, its setting. No graves mar the approach across wide, green, well-kept

One of the historical nail-studed gateways to the Cathedral Close at Salisbury showing a statue of King Edward VII gazing down at the pilgrims beneath.

lawns, set in a walled Close with houses of great beauty. This Close was first laid out in the fourteenth century, and, inevitably, some of the houses have been altered or re-built, though the whole preserved a charm and dignity that is a fine background for its focal point.

There are many houses to see — one in which Handel played, another belonging to the great merchant, Mompesson, and one on which the hand of Wren played a part in its building. (See Gazetteer for details).

One of the gates, the north, leading into the Close was embellished by a Royal Coat of Arms, having been granted a licence from Edward III when it was originally part of the fortifications.

The other side bears a statue of Edward VII to commemorate his visit to the city. An unusual feature would appear to be that the King, though suitably robed, is wearing high boots. A statue of King Charles I, wearing high boots, once stood on this site, but was destroyed by the Roundheads in the Civil War, and Edward VII 'stepped into his boots'.

Salisbury is so steeped in history, it is hard to particularise, though in 1261, Bishop Giles de Bridport established the College of St Nicholas de Vaux, England's first University, but, overshadowed by the University of Oxford, it fell into ruin.

The great market square — for Salisbury is essentially a market city, the first being held in 1222, with the right dating from 1227. It has seen much of England's history — the Duke of Buckingham was beheaded here in 1483; Lord Stourton was hung in 1556 for murdering Mr Hartgill and his son. Because of his rank, a silk cord was used for the execution, and for a time was suspended over his tomb in the Cathedral.

Markets are held here on Tuesdays and Saturdays, and at other times, the broad square is used as a car park. The Guildhall, built in the late eighteenth century was given by the Earl of Radnor to replace the Elizabethan Council House destroyed by fire. Facing the Guildhall is the fifteenth century House of John A'Port, now a china shop, but built by one of the wool merchants who was six times Mayor of Salisbury. It is a good example of a timber framed, three storeyed house with a second floor overhang and gables. It contains an Elizabethan panelled room and another room with a carved mantelpiece.

There are many old and attractive inns — the King's Arms in St John Street, facing the St Ann Gate, dates from the fifteenth century and it is remembered as the place where plans were made for the successful escape of Charles II after the Battle of Worcester. The Red Lion in Milford Street was best known in the eighteenth century as a coaching inn when the 'Salisbury Flying Machine' coach left for London nightly at 10 pm, though the inn itself is of fourteenth century origin. The Pheasant Inn in Salt Lane forms part of Crew's Hall, named after Philip Crewe and is another timber framed fifteenth century building, donated by him to the local Company of Shoemakers in 1638. It was formerly called the Crispin Inn after St Crispin, the patron saint of Shoemakers.

Close to the Square, at the end of Butcher Row, is an ancient Poultry Cross, the last remaining of four such crosses in the City. Nearby, is a very old inn — the Haunch of Venison, (which still serves the meat!)

built in the 13th century, with old oak beams and rafters and fireplaces that have delighted travellers for centuries.

The High Street, a mixture of old and modern development, uses the name of a once famous old inn, the Old George where Pepys stayed in 1668, as a modern shopping precinct, though the original fourteenth century features were retained. On the other side is Mitre House, once an inn and the reputed site on which Bishop Poore is said to have lived when building the Cathedral. Opposite is a timber framed fourteenth century bookshop — Beach's — which is a fascinating place to visit.

As a great wool centre, there is much evidence of the wealth of the city's merchants — not least the Halle of John Halle, which forms the foyer of the Odeon Cinema in the Canal. The fifteenth century banqueting hall of this merchant is a magnificent entrance for a cinema, though I always feel I should see historical films in this setting! John Halle was four times Mayor of the City and his house was built in 1470 and restored by Pugin in the nineteenth century. The Halle arms and merchant's mark can still be seen above the stone chimneys.

St Ann Street (near one of the Close gates) has a notable building — the former Joiners' Hall which dates from the sixteenth century and is said to be one of the best timber framed houses in the city. Its main feature is the wood carving at the front of the hall and the fine oriel windows. It was bought by the National Trust in 1898.

The Salisbury and South Wilts Museum in the same street is worth a visit as it contains a fine collection of relics of life in the city through the ages, and the only Giant now left in the whole of England. He stands, some twelve feet high, with dark complexion, bushy black hair and huge, staring eyes. His robes are large enough to hide his bearer when he is moved in procession through Salisbury Streets, beside him his Hob-nob or hobby horse, his sword and lantern and staff.

In medieval times, the Giant was known as St Christopher, possibly because the saint was known to have been a giant, and, as the patron saint of travellers, many believed that if they looked on his image, they would travel in safety.

Salisbury Giant belongs to a pre-Christian time linked with the Mid-summer Festival, and in the Middle Ages was appropriated by the Tailors' Guild whose patronal festival was June 24th.

The Giant's real age is not known, but there is evidence that he was in the procession led by the Mayor and Corporation to meet Henry VII and his Queen in 1496, and he was old at that time.

During the Commonwealth, when all merriment was frowned on, he remained hidden, to re-appear at the restoration of Charles II with much rejoicing. Now, the Giant and Hob-nob are really old and frail and appear only at coronations, waiting meanwhile, in quiet retirement.

In addition to the Cathedral, Salisbury has many other beautiful churches, among them the one dedicated to St Thomas à Becket. It was originally built in 1238 but the present church dates from the 15th century still retaining some of the earlier features. The tower *c.* 1400 first was detached from the church, but when the nave was re-built in the fifteenth century it was joined, and its east face bears two quarter-jacks in armour dating from 1581.

Its most famed possession is the Doom Painting over the Chancel Arch, which dates from 1400 and the architectural background is remarkable. It was covered at the time of the Reformation when Royal Arms, now over the south door, were placed over the chancel arch. For centuries, this painting was forgotten, until, in the nineteenth century, it was uncovered and restored. The painting of figures on either side of the chancel arch represent St Osmund on the south side and either St James or Compostella or a pilgrim, who caused the painting to be placed there to commemorate his safe return from a pilgrimage.

There is an interesting sixteenth century brass to John Webbe and his wife and children, to commemorate another wool merchant who was Mayor and Member of Parliament for the City.

The organ was originally presented to the Cathedral by George III but transferred to St Thomas' church in 1877.

A city such as Salisbury has many famous people associated with its history, so I have kept my list to those born within its walls.

There is a statue of Henry Fawcett in the Market Square who was born here, the son of a city shopkeeper, in 1833 and played a marked role in the political life of this country.

Fawcett studied mathematics at Cambridge, and decided to read for the Bar entering Lincoln's Inn in 1858. Then tragedy struck. One September day, he was out shooting with his father on Harnham Hill near Salisbury, when some birds flew beyond Mr Fawcett Senior's boundary. Henry moved and another covey rose. Mr Fawcett fired, blinding his son. Henry overcame his disability and decided to go into politics becoming a Professor of Political Economy. He made several attempts as a Parliamentary candidate until he was finally elected as Liberal Member for Brighton. His wife, Millicent, was also a remarkable woman in her own right. She was keenly interested in women's suffrage. Fawcett became interested in India speaking on behalf of the natives earning their respect. In fact, when he lost his seat in 1874, many Indians raised money to help him and he continued to press their case. Though he supported Gladstone, he was not given Cabinet rank when appointed to the Post Office in 1880. Some said this was because of his blindness, others that Gladstone disliked Mrs Fawcett. His administration of the Post Office brought about many changes and his re-organisation of the service laid the foundations for the modern system, particularly in the introduction of the postal order. He died in 1884 and his native city honoured him with a statue in the market square.

John of Salisbury, whose real name was Little, was born at Old Sarum between 1115 and 1120. He was always proud of his birthplace and was a fellow pupil with Becket, becoming his secretary at Canterbury when Becket became Archbishop. He was a devoted and loyal follower of the Archbishop narrowly escaping death when the murder took place at Canterbury. He had shared his Primate's exile though always longed to return to England especially to see his aged mother. In 1176 John was appointed Bishop of Chartres where he died in 1180 leaving a treasure of his writings for posterity.

The musician, Michael Wise, a native of Salisbury, was appointed Master of the Choristers and Organist of the Cathedral in 1668, and found favour with Charles II. He was appointed a gentleman of the Chapel Royal in 1675, and later Almoner and Master of Choristers of St Paul's Cathedral. He was suspended from office for offending the King, by commencing his voluntary before the sermon had ended! He returned to Salisbury, but was a man of violent nature which led to much quarrelling and was the cause of his death. In August 1687, after a row with his wife, he rushed out into the Cathedral Close. The Watch, thinking him a robber, stopped him and a scuffle ensued during which Wise received a blow on the head which fractured his skull and he lay dead before the Cathedral. A new organist was needed for the Cathedral in which he had served for years, due to his temper!

Another very well known writer who died recently lived just outside Salisbury, and it is interesting to think that John Creasey, one of the world's most prolific authors with over five hundred thrillers to his credit, chose to live in Wiltshire. He wrote prodiguously, 560 novels or 56,000,000 words in forty years and was once told he ran a 'fiction factory'. He had twenty-eight pen names and left a legacy which enriched the library world.

There are many others associated with this great city, and it has always attracted men of the arts — the first edition of Goldsmith's *Vicar of Wakefield* was printed here; Arthur Bryant has come to live in the city contributing to its annual Arts Festival which attracts the great from the arts world.

Salisbury was once known for its cutlery. It was never such a large industry locally, as, say, in Sheffield, but the local products had a reputation for fine workmanship. The industry was at its height in the nineteenth century and cutlery was exhibited for sale to passengers on the Exeter coaches and, there were ten cutlers in the city, The trade still existed in the early part of this century.

Among the legends are two connected with the Cathedral. The first, rather a sinister tale, is that curious, large birds like albatrosses with dazzling white wings (claimed by some to be angels) hover over the Bishop's Palace, their wings still as they fly, whenever a Bishop is dying.

In 1885, Miss Moberly saw them rise from the ground in the Palace Garden, just before the death of her father who was Bishop; and they were seen again by Edith Olivier when returning to the City when she heard of another Bishop's demise.

Centuries ago, St Nicholas Day, the 6th December, was observed as a great festival in the Church, and Salisbury Cathedral was no exception. Here, from among the choristers, a 'Boy Bishop' was chosen, and this mock Bishop's term of office lasted for three weeks from St Nicholas Day until the Feast of the Holy Innocents on the 28th December, during which time he enacted a series of elaborate pageants and conducted services. If he died during this time, he was buried with the full honours of a bishop. Folk tradition claims that a miniature effigy of a bishop in the cathedral is that of a boy bishop who died in office — in spite of denials by historians.

Salisbury has a very famous school on Milford Hill. The Godolphin School, founded in 1726, is one of the oldest girls' public schools in England, and its pupils are distinguished by the straw boater hat with scarlet band they wear as part of their uniform. It was founded by Elizabeth Godolphin who left money in her Will to found a school for 'eight orphan gentlewomen' and from this nucleus a great school began. Its bicentenary was celebrated in 1926 in Westminster Abbey with a special Service of Thanksgiving, and the school flourishes today, part of the City scene.

Another Wiltshire 'first' is the formation of the first Salvation Army Band by some intrepid musicians from Salisbury. Charles William Fry of the City, whose mother kept the Green Dragon at Alderbury, had three sons and together they formed the nucleus of the now world-known bands. In April 1870, they played in the Market Place for the followers of the Movement and, at first, there was much objection from the citizens who disliked a drum being played on a Sunday. Prejudice overcome the Band flourished and the Frys became keen Salvationists. A monument to the 'First Bandmaster of the Salvation Army' was unveiled in Glasgow (where he died) to Charles Fry in 1882.

Salisbury bandsmen again made history in December 1922 when the Band Vocal Quartet were the first Salvationists musicians to broadcast.

The importance of the great Plain approaching Salisbury must not be minimised, for its broad acres of open grassland so ideal for sheep, have brought prosperity to the county.

Four miles from the city is the Race Plain, and Salisbury Races, held three times a year, are among the oldest in England. The Bibury Club, formed at Bibury over the border in Gloucestershire in 1681, is thought to be the oldest racing club in the world, and was visited by Charles II on a number of occasions. The first race meeting at Salisbury was recorded in 1585, and Henry, Earl of Pembroke, who is said to have instituted the races, gave a golden bell, worth £50 to be competed for annually.

In the seventeenth century, there were two courses at Salisbury, one of fourteen miles in length which began at Whitesheet Hill and ended at Harnhill Hill, and another which was four miles long. A horse called Peacock, belonging to Sir Thomas Thynne ran the four mile course in five minutes. Queen Elizabeth I is said to have enjoyed a day's racing three months before Drake sailed to defeat the Armada in 1588.

The Bibury Club came to Salisbury in 1899 and, for many years, only its members were eligible to participate. There are, as expected, many racing stables in the area, and for years a lot of horses came from the famous Druid's Lodge stables near Stonehenge, owned by the late J.V. Rank. There are others at Shrewton, and Sir Gordon Richards (now moved into Hampshire) and several, including Jeremy Tree near Marlborough. The famous horses are legion but the great Mill Reef ran his first race there, Brigadier Gerard his second, and Tudor Minstrel was ridden there by Gordon Richards.

This wild and windy Plain offers excellent racing and wonderful views of South Wiltshire.

For centuries the silence of the springy turf on the Plain made the area round Larkhill perfect for birdsong until the noise of the modern age broke its peace.

In 1909, Larkhill became one of the first pioneer flying centres in the country when the Bristol Tramway and Carriage Company entered into the aircraft industry by creating a flying school on the Plain. It was here that the 'Boxkite' the first plane by the company's own designer, took the air in 1910. It was from one of these planes that a successful ground wireless link was achieved. An experimental tractor biplane was not so successful, it overturned into a crowd of spectators in 1912. This airfield played its part in the testing of a number of the Bristol series of aircraft used in World War I.

In September 1914, the flying school closed down and one of the new army camps took its place.

Wiltshire's coat of arms bears a strange bird — the great bustard. Once these huge birds, like great turkeys weighing up to thirty pounds, roamed freely across the plains, and in the distance they resembled sheep. But they were not nearly so easy to catch! Their wings were strong, they could move fast and were wary, cunning birds. It was the increase of agriculture that finally drove them from Wiltshire by ploughing and enclosure and by 1800 they were uncommon.

It was a sad loss — they had graced the tables of many banquets and provided a fine spectacle, so it was with pleasure that ornithologists noted, some one hundred and forty years later, that they had re-established themselves at Porton Down. Some thirteen birds appeared and it is hoped once again they will be a familiar sight on the Plain.

Though it has been said the Plain has been used by the Army since Roman times, the largest military manoeuvres the county has ever known took place at Alderbury in September 1910.

A large house party, which included the Duke of Connaught, Sir Winston Churchill, Lord Kitchener and Lord Roberts, had gathered at the country home, Wilton House, of Lord Pembroke for the occasion, and they turned out in force, with their ladies to see the excitement.

Some forty-eight thousand troops were involved, divided into opposing armies for the battle of the Plain superintended by Sir John French.

The airship *Beta* was used for military reconnaissance in this exercise, the first time an aeroplane was ever used in this way, but, unfortunately, it was forced down by a burst carburettor, though not before it made military history.

The army took time off for pleasure in the Wiltshire countryside, and in 1940 the Royal Artillery (Salisbury Plain) Hunt was established as a successor to the Royal Artillery Harriers which were formed in 1908 to hunt the southern part of the Tedworth country.

It is said to be the only recognised pack of foxhounds maintained by a Regiment in England. The kennels are at Larkhill and all the hunt staff are amateurs.

The county claims another first this time that the first tournament held in England took place at Salisbury in the reign of Richard I in 1194. Richard, needed money for his Crusades and the cost of the wars with France, so created the first system of licensed tourneying. Licence fees of 20 marks were payable for an earl; 10 marks for a baron and either 4 or 2 marks for a knight, depending whether or not he held land. To collect this tax, the king limited the tournaments to five specified places, Salisbury being one of them.

There are eight Salisburys all over the world in Zimbabwe, Australia and America among them, but, of course, Moonrakers claim *their* city is the fairest.

The Plain has many villages and the following is a selection of some of them. There are lots more, but these have particular interests.

The village of Alderbury overlooking the Avon Valley has royal connections. King Stephen founded an Augustinian Priory for his foresters, which is now covered by a farm, but traces of carvings made by the monks can be seen in the walls of the house named Ivychurch.

A mile away, Clarendon, was one of the royal palaces, starting as a hunting box for Norman kings, extending into a country house for the Plantagenets. Later, Edward III entertained two royal prisoners, John of France and David of Scotland, and the three are said to have hunted in the forests. The name of an inn — the Three Crowns, is said to have originated from this time. Henry VIIIth abandoned the palace itself. Thomas à Becket rode down the old track that still leads to it and met Henry II there, when they agreed on the sixteen points regulating the conduct of the clergy. St Thomas' path from Winterbourne to Clarendon, which is said to have been used by the saint when he was a priest at Winterbourne and came for Mass, is a miracle one, the legend being that is remains green in all seasons of the year, even when there is snow round it.

Much treasure was later discovered on this site, including the first bradawl ever used in England, an example of the earliest known window glass to be set in a lead frame, and a sculptured head, some seven hundred years old and believed to have been part of a door ornament in the king's apartment. Edward Hyde took his title from Clarendon in 1661.

On a high ridge to the south is Eyre's Folly, known by its curious shape as 'The Pepperbox'. It dates from 1606 and was the brainchild of Giles Eyre who created this hexagonal building, placed it upon the highest point on his land, and from it gazed on the whole countryside.

The Green Dragon Inn is reputed to be yet another of Dickens — 'The Blue Dragon.'

In the heart of the Wylye valley, with the river flowing through it, is another 'miracle' place. Bishopstrow, as its name implies, was once connected with a Bishop. Who else but St Aldhelm? Legend recalls that the Saint was walking here and planted his staff in the ground. It miraculously changed into an ash tree, and the place became known as 'Bishop's Treow' or the Bishop's Tree.

It has long historical associations — the Romans built a house here, the Saxons a church, though neither remain. Alfred camped here after a defeat by the Danes, and, eight hundred years later, Cromwell breakfasted under a yew tree after the Battle of Newbury.

Britford is a tiny village with a large church containing an elaborate tomb once believed to be the Duke of Buckingham who was beheaded in Salisbury Market Place in 1483, though when it was brought to the church in the eighteenth century, it contained no body.

Longford Castle, one of the county's finest houses, was built in 1591 by Sir Thomas Gorges who was interested in the occult and stands in a park of two hundred and fifty acres. Money from a wrecked Spanish Armada galleon was used for some of the building designed by John Thorpe, architect of Holland House in London. Sir Thomas' wife was a

Maid of Honour to Queen Elizabeth I. The Gorges family lived here for half a century, then it became the property of Lord Coleraine and was used in the Civil War by the Royalist cavalry. It was spared by Cromwell. In the eighteenth century, Sir Edward Bouverie, ancestor of the Earl of Radnor bought it.

Longford Castle is unusual as it was built in triangular shape, said to be emblematic of its owner's Catholic sympathies, and later remodelled in the nineteenth century by Savin. The house contains much fine furniture and paintings and the park and gardens were laid out by Capability Brown. Like Amesbury, Wilton and Longleat, Longford was built by an aristocrat with court connections and Chilmark stone used in its construction.

The Nadder Valley is a beautiful part, and, with its own stream to water it, the little village of Chilmark is world known. Quantities of fine, creamy, freestone has been quarried here for centuries to be used in many of the county (and indeed country's) houses and churches. Maybe its greatest glory is that though many of the priories built with its stone have long vanished, the stone still stands, and since Roman times there have been quarries here.

John de Chilmark, a mathematician and philosopher of the fourteenth century, called the 'Archimedes of his age' was probably baptised in the church which still retains its seven hundred year old doorway.

Triangular Longford Castle is thought to have been built in honour of the Trinity by its devout owner.

In the 1600s, people from Chilmark took ship in the *Mayflower* for America, and there is a place bearing the Wiltshire name in Massachusetts where they settled.

Downton is really one long, very wide street with, at one end the Downton Tannery with its own water wheel, and opposite a power station. This was once claimed to be the smallest in England.

There are remnants of the Saxon Meeting place known as the Moot, now an earthwork in the garden of a seventeenth century house.

Downton, which is older than Salisbury, appears in history in the seventh century as a gift from the West Saxon King to the Bishop of Winchester. A later bishop laid out the plan of the town — which remains much the same today, though all trace of his castle, or palace, has gone. This was a 'Rotten' Borough sending two Members to Parliament until the Reform Act of 1832.

In its heyday, there were two fairs, in April and October, and it was especially known for the sale of New Forest ponies. The manor was once the home of the Raleighs, Walter's brother, Carew, representing Downton in Parliament.

Among the inns, the Bull has a well-known fisherman's sign outside — a fish. This is a reminder — for the unitiated — that the name comes from a 'Bull' trout!

Nearby, at Standlynch, is Trafalgar House which was given to the nation by the descendants of Nelson.

At Farley, Sir Stephen Fox, the man alleged to have told Charles II of Cromwell's death, built a group of almshouses in 1681 in this village. He was a yeoman farmer's son who entered the Percy household as a page, and later he taught soldiering. At the Battle of Worcester he was second in command of the King's Ordnance, and accompanied his King to the Continent where he became financier of the Royal Household.

After the Restoration, he received many Royal favours and became a friend of Evelyn, Pepys and Wren. He made a great deal of money and was able to set up many churches and almshouses including the Royal Hospital in Chelsea. Farley was several times Member of Parliament for Sarum and a statesman. He lived through six reigns, almost reaching his ninetieth year. He served in the Treasury of William III and led the Commons in procession at the Coronation of Queen Anne in 1702. He is buried at Farley church where there are many memorials to his family, including one to his famous descendant, Charles James Fox, his grandson.

Oak Apple Day in Wishford is no ordinary occasion, for here May 29th is celebrated with great fervour. An old custom commemorating the rights of the villagers to cut wood in Grovely Wood has links with pre-Christian tree worship. In 1603, the villagers were granted the right

The bread stones at Great Wishford proclaim the price of bred for a hundred and seventy five years.

to gather wood for all time and they still celebrate. Everyone goes to the wood, accompanied by a band of musicians (a loose term for there is music of all and every kind) and they return to the village bearing branches marching through the streets proclaiming "Grovely, Grovely, and all Grovely. Unity is Strength.' A party then go to Salisbury Cathedral where the Rector of Wishford reads out the relevant part of the charter.

In 1629, Sir Richard Grobham, Steward of Longford Castle, lived at Wishford Manor. He was an enthusiastic hunter and one day slew a wild boar in Grovely Forest, said to have been the last man to do so. His sword and helmet were hung in the church to commemorate the event and his tomb is one of the finest of the county's seventeenth century monuments.

Stone tablets in the churchyard have proclaimed the price of bread for the last one hundred and seventy five years, and there are now seven stones, dating from 1800 to the latest, in decimal currency, added in 1971.

In the little village of Newton Tony, almost on the Hampshire border, a remarkable woman was born at the manor house (now gone) in 1662. From here she set out on horseback on many rides and recounted them all faithfully in her Journals. This celebrated woman diarist Celia Fiennes, visited many parts of England, no mean feat in the seventeenth century and her accounts of her travels are a delight to read.

THESE COTTAGES
BUILDED IN THE YEAR OF OUR LORD
1842
FROM A PORTION OF THE FUND SUBSCRIBED BY THE PUBLIC
TO REPAIR THE LOSSES SUSTAINED BY THE POOR
OF THIS AND FIVE NEIGHBOURING PARISHES IN
THE GREAT FLOOD OF
1841
ARE VESTED IN THE NAMES OF
TWELVE TRUSTEES
WHO SHALL LET THEM TO THE BEST ADVANTAGE
AND AFTER RESERVING OUT OF THE RENTS
A SUM SUFFICIENT TO MAINTAIN THE PREMISES
IN GOOD REPAIR
SHALL EXPEND THE REMAINDER IN
FUEL AND CLOTHING
AND DISTRIBUTE THE SAME AMONGST THE POOR OF THE
SAID PARISHES
ON THE 16 DAY OF JANUARY FOR EVER
BEING THE ANNIVERSARY OF THAT AWFUL VISITATION.

Shrewton, where a stream runs at the side of the main street and has been known to flood!

Odstock lies in the Ebble Valley, and is the scene of a tragic and true love story. A local gipsy, Josiah Scamp pleaded guilty to a crime committed by his son-in-law and was executed in his stead, as he did not want his beloved daughter to be a widow. The gipsies who knew his innocence paid an annual pilgrimage to his grave, and one year indulged in drunken brawls so fell foul of the Vicar. The gipsy queen cursed him and he was dead within a year. The church itself was also cursed with the saying that if the church door was locked, whoever did so would die. The curse has never been lifted, but legend recounts that the key (for safety sake) was long ago thrown into the Ebble.

There is a wood of prehistoric origin and dark yew tunnels meet at its centre. Cromwell stayed in the village.

Odstock Hospital, is well known for plastic surgery and also the nearby 'common cold' research station.

A blindhouse or lockup provides a grim reminder of olden days. It is one of thirteen still in existence in the county.

A mile away to the south is Clearbury Ring, a hill of some four hundred and sixty eight feet in height encircled by an earth rampart and topped by beeches.

One of the well known 'Plain' villages is Shrewton which, in days long gone, must have been a welcome sight to travellers crossing the lonely downland.

A stream runs down the side of the main street which, in the Great Flood of 1841, overflowed its banks causing terrible damage and the re-building of many cottages, seen in a modernised row, with an inscription telling the dreadful tale.

A blind lockup, one of many in the county, used to stand near the bridge, and this has been moved brick by brick for road widening, but without visible change. Prisoners were confined here before being taken to the gibbet, half a mile away for execution. A forbidding clump of trees still marks the spot.

It is a pleasant village, a gentle one undisturbed by the rattle of army vehicles that pass its streets, and where ducks still swim in the cool waters of the stream, and flowers grow beside the houses in a delightful decoration.

Further south, on the borders of Dorset, is a beautiful village known as Tollard Royal and once beloved of Kings who came for the hunting in the nearby Cranborne Chase, part of which is in Wiltshire and part over the border. King John was especially fond of this place and spent much time here. He granted it a charter in the 13th century, and his house, some of it of that period, is a delight in wood and stone combining to give a truly medieval air.

The ancient larmer tree — a wych elm — was the site of meetings of the Court Leet and, by tradition, the place where the king met his huntsman before a chase.

A marble tablet in the church commemorates (in 1900) the archaeologist, General Pitt-Rivers who lived near, and did so much to excavate and discover the ways of life of our ancestors. The story is that, as a soldier in the Crimea, he was struck by the evolution of weapons, and made a study of tools and weapons of all ages. His vast collections and findings are in the nation's treasure houses and there is much of his evidence to be found at the Farnham Museum over the border.

West Dean is a hilly village with a stream. Its great house has gone, but the family name remains in the Chantry Chapel built in 1333 by Robert de Borbach. There are many monuments to the Pierreponts and the Evelyns, including one charming brass to George Evelyn, who died at the age of six in 1641. This resembles a Van Dyck portrait!

Wilsford cum Lake is a hamlet with a chequered house built by a clothier, George Duke, who bought the estate in 1578. It fell into decay

Lake House, Wilsford is of sixteenth century origin, but rebuilt after being gutted by fire.

and was restored by Detmar Blow in 1898. Another Duke, Edward, who was a great discoverer of antiquities lived there and was much concerned with the burial mounds on his estate. He believed that the early inhabitants had devised the monuments as a vast planetarium.

Sir Oliver Lodge who lived at Lake House, died there at the age of ninety. He is buried in the church, and was one of the pioneers of the Wireless Age. It was on the basis of his coherer that Marconi built up the wireless system and made broadcasting a reality.

Winterslow is a hill village said to have been continuously inhabited since Roman times, and is mainly known for its inn, the Pheasant, reached after a wonderful, exhilarating journey across the downs.

Perhaps its most famous time was in October 1816, at that time known as the Winterslow Hut, when a travelling menagerie was parked in the forecourt of the inn and, as the Exeter Mail Coach drew up, one of the leading horses was pounced on by a lioness which had escaped. Panic ensued, the passengers ran into the safety of the inn, but the coachman and the guard — perhaps too scared to move — stayed on their high seats, though, in fairness, the guard did try to shoot the lion with his blunderbuss. A gallant Newfoundland dog grabbed the lion by a paw but was badly mauled and the lion hid among the staddle stones supporting the granary. The menagerie owner, fearing to lose his valuable animal, showed great courage by crawling under the granary, and eventually they secured the lion.

The horse, whose name was Pomegranate, was on show, with all her wounds, at Salisbury Fair the next day. Legend says that one of the passengers was so terrified when the lioness brushed against him in his wild rush for the door that he went mad!

It was in this inn that William Hazlitt stayed and wrote many of his essays. His wife had property near and he loved to walk to Stonehenge and listen for the sound of the bugle that heralded the arrival of the mail coach.

The Holland family tried to create a park and mansion here, but after two attempts destroyed by fire, they gave up and returned to London. The Poore family, here in the last century, established a Land Court, which reclaimed common land and leased it.

In the reign of Elizabeth I, a Spaniard was said to have settled in the village, bringing with him some rather special dogs. These animals were trained to smell out the underground tuber-like fungus of the truffles which became a great delicacy.

Poodle dogs were said to be particularly adept at sniffing out the truffles, and a local character, Eli Collins was a very well-known expert in the field, his family practising their craft for generations, until they gave up in the 1930s. Eli was said to wear a special uniform provided by the Earl of Radnor.

In 1860, the truffle hunters petitioned that their dogs be exempted from the twelve shilling tax. Oak trees were good places to find, and terrier dogs became very proficient at searching. One method of locating them was to watch a particular tree, where they were suspected, and, if a swarm of small yellow flies hovered, it was worth digging.

And this place, so steeped in history and legend has its very own witch! Liddie Shears, who lived in about 1810, was reputed to be a witch, and it was said that, if the local poachers did not take her some snuff or baccy (protection money) there would be no hares to catch. If the 'dues' were paid, old Liddie would go round the fields at night with a flint and steel to cause sparks which made the hares sit up.

Her cottage was a lonely one and local people were said to be in dread of her. Farmer Tanner, who lived near, kept a stud of greyhounds for coursing, and passed her cottage often, always asking where he could find hares. She told him, and the hare was always there, but was also always lost at the back of her cottage. The farmer was puzzled so asked the Rector for advice. He suggested that a bullet was made of a sixpence and then the hare be shot within sight of the cottage. This was done and the hare shot dead as it entered the garden.

Later, Farmer Tanner called at the cottage. There was no sign of the hare, but Liddie Shears lay dead on the floor. It was found that a silver bullet had caused her death.

So, if you go walking at night in the fields of this village, watch out for sparks in case they are the ghost of Liddie Shears!

2

Avebury, Silbury, Marlborough and the valley of the Kennet villages, and on to Swindon and district

One of the most important early Bronze Age Temples in Europe, Avebury is world known, and the earliest structures date back to 2,500 B.C. in the late Neolithic Age. The huge, standing stones represent one of the largest henge monuments left today, and it is considered older than Stonehenge from where some of the famous Avebury Circle stones came.

Whichever way one approaches the village, one soon becomes aware of the stones, for they stretch out along both sides of the main road, looking as natural as trees. Yet there is *something* about them that makes one pause. To some, they represent something sacred and a feeling of awe pervades, for however many tourists come to stare and photograph, there is always peace at Avebury. It is that sort of place.

There are now some ninety-eight stones, some weighing over thirty tons, in a great circle, the whole enclosing some twenty-eight acres. Part of the fascination lies in the fact that, within the huge Circle, is the greater part of a village, and attractive cottages, some thatched, were originally constructed from the stones removed from the Circle itself. At first, there were two or three smaller circles within the great Circle, parts of which can still be seen. Today it is impressive, when complete it must have been an awe-inspiring sight.

The sarsen stones — which make up the Circle, derive their name from medieval times when many felt they had magical properties, and connected with legends brought back by the Crusades of the Saracens who were said to have been powerful magicians. The stones have a strange quality and can give a small electric shock when rubbed, which has led to many superstitions and folklore.

Avebury village has been continuously occupied for more than a thousand years, and it is believed it was once a great religious centre, for there is evidence of grass trackways which links up every part of

Britain. At the spread of Christianity, the Saxons built a church outside the ancient temple, the Normans added to it and later a tower was built in the fifteenth century. The Saxon font is a great treasure, and the church now possesses an unusual brass, that of a priest, brought here from the redundant church of Berwick Bassett where it had been since 1427.

John Aubrey paid a visit in 1646 and first 'noticed' the place, but William Stukeley mentioned the two rings of stones in 1743 in his book, noting that many of the stones were destroyed to make land for ploughing. Great restoration was carried out from 1934 to 1939 by the late Alexander Keiller (of marmalade fame) who lived in the Manor at that time. It was due to his efforts that stones which had lain buried for centuries were dug up, and, as far as possible, replaced in their original positions, the missing ones marked with concrete blocks. The bones of a fourteenth century man were discovered buried under one of the huge stones, and his scissors and coins are preserved in the museum. It was believed he was a barber-surgeon or a tailor. For a time, while the village was the scene of a television series, *Children of the Stones* the Circle was completed with the use of plastic stones, but these have been removed.

The Elizabethan Manor House has been continuously occupied for four hundred years, and before this a Priory stood on the site, founded

Avebury's Elizabethan Manor House is rich in history spanning four hundred years.

The old cider press in the forecourt of the Red Lion at Avebury makes a good talking point.

in 1110, which was given to Sir John Sherington, the Master of the Bristol Mint, on the Dissolution. For years, it was owned by Sir Francis Knowles of the family related by marriage to Elizabeth I. There is much to see — fine gardens with topiary, peacocks on the lawns, a sixteenth century dovecote (with doves!) and an eighteenth century wishing well, and, of course, it is reputedly haunted. One story goes that a maid saw a 'monk in the library' and asked if he wanted lunch and he disappeared! A seventeenth century armillary sundial is an unusual feature in the centre of the lawn, with a second on the east lawn.

The Red Lion Inn, facing the Circle, is a delightful old thatched pub with a cider press in the forecourt and a deep, 80 feet, well in one of the dining rooms. In a fascinating old village, this is certainly one place not to be missed, though beware if you are late at night for a ghostly coach is said to draw up outside, though no one has seen it. As the pub was once on the old coach road, it is not surprising, and maybe the driver is still trying to make up time!

A mile and a half north west of Avebury is Windmill Hill, some 613 feet high, and the site of the earliest Neolithic culture in Britain.

As one turns away from Avebury and back on to the Marlborough road, the first place one sees is an old pub called the Waggon and Horses Beckhampton. This has its own barrow in the garden, serves wonderful food and is featured in Dickens' 'Bagman's Tale' in *Pickwick Papers*. Once the favourite stopping place for drovers and waggoners, it is now a must for other travellers and the reputation of its food has spread far.

Within sight of this ancient hostelry, the strange, brooding and somehow majestic shadow of Silbury Hill rises, a little surprisingly, to a height of one hundred and thirty feet. It stands a little way back from the road amid a host of grey wethers — the sarsen stones with which the fields are scattered.

Some claim it is another of the county's ancient religious centres. It is largest man-made mound in Europe, and covers an area of some five miles, with a diameter of just over a hundred feet across its flat top. It is believed to have been built about 2,600 B.C. though its actual purpose has never been determined.

A popular theory suggests a burial mound for a King Sil who is said to have been placed there, on horseback, and others think there is a lifesize figure in solid gold, or a king in a golden coffin, but many excavations have revealed nothing.

At one time, many felt it was an evil place, a construction of the Devil, who was said to have dropped it while on his way to Devizes, and black magic was believed to have been practised there. In 1849, a stone circle was found, giving some substance to this theory, and, thinking the best way to be rid of evil was to bury it, this was done. Excavations carried out in 1968, revealed some isolated boulders, but nothing of significance.

Kings and Queens have stopped, like other mortals, to climb this strange hill and enjoy the fine view of the Marlborough downland beneath. Charles II and his brother, James, climbed to the top, but Queen Catherine stayed in her coach!

An old custom, which has died out, was that on Palm Sunday, all the villagers from round about, visited the hill, singing and dancing and feasting on figs and cider.

In the surrounding fields are many tracks and barrows, the whole landscape having a frosting of hundreds of sarsen stones. About half a mile from the main road, at Fyfield, is a ruined monument known as 'The Devil's Den'. It is the remains of a chambered long barrow dating back to *c.* 3,500 B.C. and is said to be haunted. The devil is claimed to appear, occasionally, at midnight, with a team of white oxen to pull it down, but so far he has not succeeded!

On the opposite side of the road is the largest monument of its kind in Britain — the West Kennet longbarrow. It was partly excavated in 1859 and again a century later.

This huge tomb, which is open to the public, is covered by a coffin-shaped mound, some three hundred and thirty feet long and eighty feet wide, and dated about 2,500 B.C. It is one of the finest Neolithic long-barrows in this country, with five burial chambers and the pillars and capstones made of sarsen stone. At least forty-six people had been buried there, men, women and children, and the pottery found suggests they were of the Beaker period, and the tomb had been in use for more

Silbury Hill, the largest man made mound in Europe has intrigued kings and commoners for many centuries.

44

than a thousand years. It would seem, from the great care taken in the preparation, that the burial chamber was an important place to which pilgrimages were made, and there is evidence that religious ceremonies were held on the site.

Local legend claims that at sunrise on the longest day of the year, the tomb is entered by a priest who is followed by a huge, white hound with red ears, though I have never been there at that time to find out!

Marlborough is approached on three sides by descending a steep hill, and the town itself, noted for its wide High Street with a church at each end, is in the valley.

This 'small and ancient borough' as it used to be called, has a history going back to prehistoric times, and has its own, smaller Silbury Hill — the Mound — in the grounds of the College. This Mound has played a

The West Kennet longbarrow the largest monument of its kind in Britain, which is open to the public and is rich in legend and history.

Inside the West Kennet longbarrow.

great part in the town's history, and can most easily be seen from the Town Hall steps, peeping above the College buildings with its trees on top, or from Granham Hill.

Merlin has a strong connection with Marlborough. Indeed, the name of the town is said to be a derivation of his name, and the motto on the Borough Arms asks, 'Where now are the bones of wise Merlin?'

A castle stood on the Mound from the eleventh century and the coins of William I were minted there. Many Norman and Plantagenet King came, particularly for the hunting in the forest, and tradition says that King John was married in the Castle Chapel of St Nicholas, and his children baptised in the huge, black font, now at Preshute Church in the town.

Henry III summoned Parliament to the Castle Precincts in 1267

The wide, sloping High Street at Marlborough, the centre of the town has a church at both ends, and the houses and shops provide a variety of architectural styles.

when the Statute of Marlborough, embodying some of the demands of Simon de Montfort, and giving rights to the smaller landowners, was passed — tradition claims on the site of what is now the Merlin Restaurant.

Time passed and the Castle declined, particularly during the Wars of the Roses, and its key is now in the possession of the College. In 1621 the Seymour family built a mansion on the site, and in 1700 this mansion became the Castle Inn (of Stanley Weyman novel fame) which flourished in the heyday of the stagecoach.

Marlborough's fine High Street, said by some to be the finest in England, is its main feature, and though there are other roads of interest, it forms the centre of the town.

During the Commonwealth, Marlborough was declared a national

47

disaster, for, in April 1653, fire broke out in the shop of a tanner (now Vincent Head) and spread so quickly that soon the south side was an inferno. 'The fire came with such force and vehemence the like was never seen in England before' said one contemporary report, and some two hundred and fifty houses were destroyed, three hundred families made homeless and damage estimated at seventy thousand pounds.

Cromwell, remembering how the town supported him in the Civil War (the Castle was for the King) ordered relief church collections throughout the country, and within a year, the town was largely rebuilt. They did not learn and two more fires in 1679 and 1690 resulted in an Act of Parliament forbidding the use of thatched roofs in Marlborough.

In spite of the conflagration, much survived, some of the buildings dating from Tudor times, making the High Street a happy blend of past and present, with Georgian buildings nestling with Elizabethan ones. A bookshop of this period (the White Horse) has a side passage leading to Back Lane, once known as Horse Passage. In days gone by, it made a good escape route for thieves robbing merchants in the markets and fairs in the main street!

The best way to see Marlborough is on foot and to walk along one side of the High Street, up the hill on to the Green with its Georgian Houses and said to be the site of a Saxon settlement, and where Sheep Fairs were held until 1893, and then back along the other side. You will find much of interest — the mixing of old and new — and do not walk too quickly or you will miss a treasure. Take a guide with you — or buy *A History of Marlborough* by Jess Chandler, one of its sons, which is fascinating reading. You will discover the meaning of many place-names — Blowhorn Street, where the herdsmen blew to inform people to look to their cattle; Blind Lane which led to nowhere and others named after the town's worthy citizens. In George Lane is a seventeenth century blacksmith's shop which is still a working smithy today.

Near the College is Ivy House, one a boys' school, owned by a Mr Greazley, whose pupils, in 1804, cut a White Horse on Granham Hill which is their memorial today.

The traditional Mop (or Hiring) Fairs are held in the High Street in October each year, the consequent disruption part of the town's life, and ordinary weekly markets also still take place.

But of course the dominating feature of Marlborough is, of course, the great Public School, founded in 1843. The Castle Inn, whose trade declined with the coming of the railways, became a school for the sons of clergymen, and Marlborough College is now one of the great Public Schools of England. In 1702, Celia Fiennes, watched the original building, now 'C' House, being built, and there are other parts to see when it is open to the public, among them, the Mount House, once an

Inn, now a Museum dating from 1744 and said to be haunted.

Since its inception, thousands of boys have come and gone, and there have been many famous Masters, among them, perhaps the best remembered being Dr Cotton, who came from Rugby steeped in Dr Arnold's traditions.

Though there may have been rivalry between College and town, they have long learned to live with each other, and still play a full part in the life of Marlborough in every sense, many serving as Mayors and Councillors.

There is much in the long history of Marlborough to remember with its Castle, religious houses, including a Gilbertine House in 1148 and its sons are among the famous. Among them — Dr Sacheverell, the notorious clergyman, was born in the Rectory in 1674; Cardinal Wolsey ordained priest at St Peter's in March 1498; Thomas Hancock, inventor of the process of India Rubber manufacture was born here in 1786 and his brother, Walter, inventor of the steam road engine in 1799.

Marlborough had its own Races on Barton Down from 1771 to 1773 and on the Common from 1840 to 1887.

Marlborough possesses an air of serenity and tranquillity, pursuing its unhurried path, untroubled by outside problems. The College gives an academic lead, almost like a small University, and the blend of town and school is an excellent one. Marlborough is a town that has endured and one can feel confident will continue to do so.

Marlborough College, part of which was the Castle Inn, a mecca for travellers, became a public school in 1843.

This huge, centuries old, hollow elm believed to have been part of Savernake Forest dominates the village of Ramsbury.

A mile or two from Marlborough one reaches the village of Mildenhall — called locally 'Minall'. This is an old place and a Roman road once linked up with Old Sarum and Cirencester here. South east is the site of the Roman town of Cunetio which has been much excavated. A Celtic Vessel, called the 'Marlborough Bucket' was discovered at Folly Farm and is now in Devizes Museum.

The Church was described by Sir John Bejteman as a 'country church which neither Victorians nor our own generation has touched'. It is like looking at a scene from a Jane Austen novel, with high box pews, special Squire's pew, two three-decker pulpits and an hour-glass by the pulpit desk. It is worth a tiny detour to see for yourself.

Ramsbury or Ravensburg (Raven's fortified place), more like a small town than a village, is dominated by a huge, centuries-old hollow elm, believed to have once been part of Savernake Forest. It is twenty-one feet in circumference.

Once a place of historical activity and one of the seats of the

Wiltshire Bishopric in the tenth century, the See was transferred to Old Sarum in 1075, but, in 1974, the Bishopric was revived and there is, once again, a Bishop of Ramsbury.

The Manor, in parkland flanking the river, was designed by John Webb, son-in-law of Inigo Jones, and there are other fine houses, including one named Parliament Piece. There is a restaurant, the Bleeding Horse, once an old coaching inn, whose name derives from the days when travelling vets lodged there, and the Bell, the inn on the square is also old and welcoming.

As ever, the church is one of the main features — very impressive and built on Saxon foundations. A ninth century cross shaft depicts a serpent biting its tail, executed in Viking style.

The most famous tombs, now stripped of their brasses, are of the Darrell family of Littlecote a mile or so away.

This fine house, steeped in history and legend, is the only major brick mansion in the county, and was built in Tudor times.

Belonging to the Wills family, this attractive house was the scene of a horrifying murder and resultant haunting. Three of its ghosts have their origin in the same story which began in November 1575. Mrs Barnes, the local midwife, was blindfolded and called to the house to attend a woman in labour. As soon as the child was delivered, a 'man of haughty and ferocious countenance' seized the baby from the midwife, and, in spite of the mother's piteous cries, pushed it deep into the red-hot

Littlecote, an Elizabethan manor house has a rich tale to unfold of murder, hauntings and an unusual relic of Cromwellian days, a chapel of the period.

embers of the fire with the heel of his boot. Mrs Barnes cut a piece of cloth from the bedhanging and it was this evidence that brought William Darrell to trial for murder. Some say that by bribing the judge, Sir John Popham (whose family subsequently owned the house) Darrell evaded punishment. But his own end was violent enough. His horse shied, maybe frightened by the ghost of the 'Burning Baby' and he was thrown and killed. Darrell's Stile as the spot came to be known is still said to be haunted by his ghost and that of his hounds, where horses still shy.

And there are other ghosts — the room in which the child died has a 'sad-looking woman', a woman, believed to be Mrs Leybourne Popham walks the gardens, a lady with a rushlight is seen, and some claim that a tenant, Gerard Bevin, who lived there after the Great War and went to prison for embezzlement, haunts the Long Gallery.

But it is the house — one of my favourites in Wiltshire — which is filled with interest. Many august persons have lived there, one of them Sir John Popham, Lord Chief Justice of England, whose family held the property until 1922. To him is attributed one of the curiosities, a finger pillory, which is still to be seen. It was used for correcting unruly prisoners in the dock, or even for the punishment of servants, and must have been very painful.

The Great Hall has true magnificence, measuring some forty-six feet by twenty-four and twenty-five feet high, and panelled all round. Henry VIII is said to have brought Jane Seymour here and one of the south windows has their initials.

In the Civil War, Colonel Alexander Popham was a Roundhead and garrisoned his officers at the house. The buff uniform coats and armour hanging on the walls are unique. To his credit, Colonel Popham was later one who aided General Monk to restore Charles II to the throne, and the King dined in the house in 1663 after pardoning the owner. Colonel Popham left his shovel board table, thirty feet long and said to be the longest of its kind, and the playing discs, bearing his initials are still preserved.

In a house filled with treasure and excitement, there is much much more to see, but perhaps the most unusual feature is the Cromwellian Chapel, believed to be the only example of such a chapel in existence today. There is no altar, but an elevated pulpit stands in its place. This simple, plain Chapel has an air of peace and unvarnished, real worship within its walls.

I always leave Littlecote with regret, yet knowing I shall come again. It is that sort of house.

And so on to a peaceful village, protected by hills on three sides. Aldbourne, for me, is a special place a 'typical country village' complete with duckpond, village green, ancient cross, old church and village

Aldbourne, a lovely village complete with Church, pubs, old cross and duckpond all cloistering round a village green is rich in history.

pump — aware of its attractions, yet not boastful.

There is evidence of continual occupation since the Bronze Age, with the population of two thousand remaining constant for many years, giving an air of solidarity and reliability.

To complete the scene, the fifteenth century church has much to offer — splendid monuments to the Walrond brothers whose life-span was one hundred and eighty years; a painted memorial to Thomas Goddard in sixteenth century armour and a brass of his ancestor, Richard, who gave the bells, dated 1462, and one of a priest of 1508, with a later incised alabaster tomb to a rector in the sixteenth century. A 'modern' touch is given by 'Adam and Eve' two eighteenth century fire waggons which, having done their duty for years, take their ease here.

There are several pubs, one, the Blue Boar goes back to 1460, and, legend relates that, in 1516, No 8 bell was upturned and filled with ale at the inn when it was dedicated. The Crown was an eighteenth century staging post, and ostlers' rooms and mounting block are still there.

The village, known for its fairs and markets, was also a working one, having, at one time, a flourishing bell foundry, known throughout the county. When this industry declined, others took its place — thatching, hurdle making and so on.

The Chase, a long, elevated trough running from Liddington to Aldbourne, once the favourite hunting ground of King and Dukes (John of Gaunt had a hunting lodge at Upper Upham) is a beautiful place. It was the scene of a skirmish in the Civil War.

Aldbourne is solid, proud of its long history. Perhaps the story of one of its sons typifies its continuing, unhurried progress. Robert Drewe, who was born here, served in the 20th Foot in the Peninsular War, in New Orleans in the American War of Independence, and then was sent to St Helena to guard Napoleon.

At over six feet in height, he was a pall bearer at his prisoner's funeral, then, duty done, he came home to Aldbourne. Each week he walked to Hungerford to collect his pension. One day, on the way home, he sat by the wayside and quietly died.

A short drive to the northwest, brings one to Swindon which is Wiltshire's largest, highest and main industrial centre. People have lived here since Neolithic times and there is evidence of Roman settlements.

It was once known as Chipping Swindon — and, rather unkindly — 'Swinedon' because of its agricultural fame, particularly pig-keeping, though, as a market town it was noted for its cheese. A quarry was found in the seventeenth century, but it was in the 1840s when the old Great Western Railway line reached Swindon that its life changed completely.

These railway cottages were built for the workers in Swindon in the last century when the railways had their heyday.

Swindon's Wyvern Theatre was opened in 1971 and visited by the Queen and Duke of Edinburgh.

Legend says that Daniel Gooch, the railway apprentice in George Stephenson's workshop, whom Isambard Kingdom Brunel chose as Superintendent of the G.W.R. and the great engineer picked the site of the new railway works while having a picnic. Brunel threw a sandwich and, there it landed, was the site of the first building!

The first line of three hundred cottages for the railway workers were laid out on the south side by 1842, and it became the 'railway' town by the provision of schools, a hospital and St Mark's Church, in 1845, for the workers.

The railway is still important, and the coming of the M4 motorway has increased the industrial power of the town. In 1962, Swindon opened a railway museum for posterity engines, railway impedimenta, including Brunel's drawing board and plans, and the furnishings of Queen Victoria's railway coach.

It was one of the first towns to inaugurate an Arts Centre and there is the flourishing modern Burnel Centre complex with the Wyvern Theatre which opened in 1971, and was visited by the Queen and Duke of Edinburgh. Sometimes, rehearsals are held outside in Theatre Square which is a great treat for spectators!

Swindon became a Borough later than most of Wiltshire's towns, in

1900, the Queen (then Princess Elizabeth) coming to its Jubilee celebrations in 1950. In the local government re-organisation of 1974, it was incorporated into the new Borough of Thamesdown, though still keeping its identity. Swindon will always be Swindon.

For all its industrialisation and commerce, Swindon numbers among its best-known sons two writers. Richard Jefferies, the son of a Wiltshire farmer, was born at Coate in 1848 and educated at Swindon. A keen naturalist, he spent much of his youth wandering on the beautiful downland, and his descriptions of them brought him great fame. His life was marred by poverty and ill-health, he enriched his county by his writing and though he died in Sussex, there is a marble bust to his memory in Salisbury Cathedral.

I think he would be delighted that the house in which he was born at Coate is now a memorial museum (full of fascinating things!) and Coate Water, where he often walked, is a popular leisure centre.

The other writer is, of course, Alfred Williams, known as the 'hammerman poet' because he worked in the railway works. He was born at South Marston, one of a family of eight, and life was hard. He wrote a great deal and was encouraged by Robert Bridges, the Poet Laureate, before joining the army in 1914. He saw service in India of which he wrote on his return to Wiltshire. Ill-health dogged him and he died without deriving benefit from the Civil List pension granted by the Prime Minister, but his writings live on.

Among the villages roundabout Swindon, is Wootton Bassett — its name the woodland run or farm — once belonged to the Bassett family. One of its unusual features is the Town Hall which stands in the middle of the main street. It is said to have been provided by Lawrence Hyde in 1700 and extensively restored by Sir Henry Meux in 1889. It is a half-timbered building supported by fifteen stone columns and reached by an open staircase.

The first Sir Winston Churchill, father of the first Duke of Marlborough, had a house near the town hall. And there is another of Wiltshire's white horses, cut in 1864, nearby.

Three miles from Swindon is Lydiard Tregoze, a village with a history dating from Saxon times.

Henry St John, Viscount Bolingbroke, the Tory statesmen was born here, but the 'famous' St Johns were the lords of the manor in the Civil War, supporting their King, three sons dying of wounds. The church contains fine memorials, and was enlarged by the family in the fifteenth century. In 1633 Sir John St John made a mortuary chapel for his family including an elaborate triptych with hinged, painted panels which open to reveal life-size painted figures of Sir John and his wife. But perhaps the dominating figure is the 'Golden Cavalier' — Edward St John who was killed in 1645, and still stands, shining to this day.

The Golden Cavalier, Edward St John, who was killed in the Civil War, stands out in Lydiard Tregoze Church which is remarkable for its monuments.

The house at Lydiard Park was re-built by another John St John in 1743 and is a splendid classical building which is open to the public.

Highworth is, as its name suggests, on top, and from it you can see for three counties.

There are some good houses, many dating from the seventeenth century when the Civil War brought its troubles to the town. The church held out for the king, but was captured by Fairfax, many of the dead being buried in a field nearby.

The Warneford family are prominent here with many memorials in the church, among them one of Lieutenant R.A.J. Warneford, V.C. who shot down the first Zeppelin to be destroyed in flight in the first World War.

A war heroine of the Second World War was also a native of Highworth. Mrs Mabel Stranks, who died at the age of eighty-eight, played an important role in the Resistance Movement, when, as local sub-postmistress, she would telephone to agents engaged in secret service. Her name was said to have been on Hitler's death list, should the Germans have invaded this country.

Cricklade is specially known as Wiltshire's only town on the banks of the River Thames, and for possessing a church whose tower is a landmark for miles. It is dedicated to St Sampson, a Breton Saint, born in 465 and, whose legend claims, presided over a school here.

This was a Roman settlement, Alfred was here, and a London goldsmith, Robert Jenner, founded a school in 1651. Beyond the church a group of houses, known as the Priory, incorporate the remains of the thirteenth-century hospital of St John the Baptist.

Broad Hinton church is worth a visit for its monuments, one to a blasphemer! Sir Thomas Wroughton and his family, kneeling in prayer, are shown in a sixteenth-century tomb. Legend says that he returned from hunting to find his wife reading a Bible instead of cooking his supper. Furious, he threw the Bible on to the fire, and his wife rescued it, but her hands were burnt. As a punishment, Sir Thomas' hands and those of his four children withered away, and the monument shows all five without hands.

There is a standing alabaster figure to Colonel Francis Glanville, killed fighting for the king, shown in full armour, with his own real armour displayed above him. While the colonel was fighting for his king, Sir John Glanville was burning down the manor house to save it from the Roundheads. He was Speaker of the Short Parliament. The Duke of Wellington held the manor for the last two years of his life.

On a modern note, Lyneham, which was once an obscure village, is now world known since it became an R.A.F. base in 1940, and is now the largest in England, the jumping off (or arriving) place for many distinguished travellers.

3

Bradford-on-Avon, Melksham, Trowbridge, Box and some weavers' towns and villages in the west

'Bradford of the Saxons' as some called it, is so different from many other Wiltshire towns that some say its architecture seems to be part of the City of Bath over the border!

Called a 'melody of stone,' the town stands on a steep hill with the River Avon flowing into the valley, it was originally one of the great weaving towns of Wiltshire, its Flemish weavers coming here in the reign of Edward III. The clothing industry has long disappeared, forced by the machine age to close its mills, though, to be fair, they continued until 1905 when rubber took the place of wool as the main industry. The clothiers left a rich heritage in their wake for there is much to see in this town.

Obviously, one of its main attractions must be the tiny Saxon Church of St Lawrence, built one thousand years ago and now the only complete Saxon Church in England. The church is believed to have been built by St Aldhelm and called 'the purest Saxon Church in England', it stands, stark and bare, almost naked in its simplicity. It is as tall as it is long and twice as high as it is wide, with its chancel arch, the narrowest in the country, only three feet six inches in width. The church lay hidden and forgotten for centuries until it was 'discovered' through the patience of Canon Jones, Vicar of Bradford in the 1850s who saw signs of its existence. In 1871 his dreams were realised and it was possible to separate the church from the surrounding buildings and it is now preserved as an ancient monument.

The 'modern' church is of Norman origin and was much restored in the last century. It contains some interesting memorials — a fine brass to Anne Longe and to Thomas Horton and his wife. He was one of the wool merchants who brought prosperity to the town, and his memorial bears his merchant's mark. The brass also has no date of death, either for Thomas Horton or his wife. He died in 1530 and built the original

The tiny Saxon Church of St Lawrence at Bradford-on-Avon is moving in its simplicity.

Old Church House which, in 1859, was used as a cloth factory, and is standing today.

There is another memorial to the Shrapnel family who lived in the town for three generations, the last being Zachariah Shrapnel in 1796, and was the father of the famous Lieutenant General Henry Shrapnel who died on the 13th March 1842.

This remarkable man served in the Royal Artillery in Flanders, and invented the shrapnel shell in 1785 which was adopted by the army in 1803, and commended by Wellington in the Peninsula and Waterloo. He lived at Midway Manor a mile or so from Wingfield. The gateway of his house is topped by shrapnel bombs and the names of battles won by its use are commemorated — Waterloo, Table Bay, Chuzneemedanse, Kioze, Bidasoa, Tsage and Busaco.

In 1001, Bradford was given to the Abbey of Shaftesbury and, early in the fourteenth century, a huge tithe barn was built. It is one of the largest existing in England, in excellent condition, and was given to the nation by the Wiltshire Archaeological Society. It is 55 yards long, 10 yards wide with 14 great bays and 4 projecting gables porches. The sturdy timbers bear up the span of the roof which extends over 10,000 square feet, and the roof tiles, over, 30,000 in number, weigh about a hundred tons. You can get to the barn by Burton Bridge — a fourteenth century pack horse bridge.

Midway Manor showing the gateposts topped by shrapnel bombs at the home of their inventor who fought under Wellington at Waterloo and gave them his name.

This fourteenth century tithe barn at Bradford-on-Avon is one of the largest still in England, and belongs to the nation.

One of the town's most photographed features is the town bridge which was originally a thirteenth century pack horse bridge, enlarged in the 15th century with nine arches and a fourteenth century chapel which was converted to a lockup in the seventeenth century. This blind house has a domed roof with a weather vane shaped like a fish. There is a local saying 'under the fish and above the water' describing occupants of the lockup.

There are many seventeenth and eighteenth century houses as well as industrial Georgian buildings. The Swan Hotel is a pleasant one, its Georgian exterior being added to an earlier one. Behind is the Bullpit, the scene of bull baiting in medieval times.

The Hall is a fine Elizabethan building built by John Hall about 1610. It is a country house in character, and was the model for the British exhibit in the Paris Exhibition of 1900. The grounds may be seen by appointment.

Bradford is a place of underground streams and water perpetually tumbled from Ladywell, once the only source of water, apart from the river. There is a medieval shopping area known as 'The Shambles' and many antique shops, teashops and a great deal to see.

Obviously its history developed through the clothing industry and Paul Methuen was among the first to bring Dutch weavers to England in the seventeenth century, establishing them in Dutch Barton. Today, the name of Alex Moulton is world known for his invention of the Moulton bicycle and the then revolutionary Hydrolastic car suspension.

Another modern industry, yet not so well known, is that of mushroom mining which began in some disused limestone quarries just before the First World War when a French family settled in Bradford. Mushrooms from here are sold all over, and the workers toil for three hundred and sixty four days a year — the only exception being Christmas Day — in order to tend the special mushrooms.

A happy harmony of old and new, Bradford has a rich inheritance with many houses of distinction, though it has kept pace with modernity, in no way, has it lost faith with its history.

South Wraxall Manor, a blend of Elizabethan and Jacobean architecture, has been the home since the fifteenth century of the Long family, another of the great merchants of the county. Tradition says that it is here that Sir Walter Raleigh, a friend of Sir Walter Long, first smoked their pipes becoming the first two smokers in England, and a Raleigh room commemorates the event.

Another delightful manor is Great Chalfield with its church approached through the gateway of the manor. It was built in 1480,

The Hall at Bradford-on-Avon was built in 1610 and was later the model for the British exhibit at the Paris exhibition of 1900.

The early Tudor Manor House at Great Chalfield was built by Thomas Tropenell in 1480 in the Wars of the Roses, and is an excellent example of a late medieval English manor house.

during the Wars of the Roses by Thomas Tropenell, and is described as one of the most perfect examples of a late medieval English manor house. The approach is different, too, for the house is moated, and much of its attraction lies in the yellowish-grey Corsham stone of which it was built.

In the dining room is a portrait of the builder, Thomas Tropenell, who sat as Member of Parliament for Bedwyn and Bath, resembling a Chinese mandarin as he sits grasping the arms of his chair!

The house was garrisoned by Parliamentary forces during the Civil War and withstood a short siege from the Royalists. It is now the property of the National Trust.

Melksham, is one of Wiltshire's smaller towns, and, like so many others, weavers plied their trade here. In 1818 the discovery of a spring led to attempts at making in a spa, but competition from Bath was too strong.

For its size, it is very industrialised with the great Avon Rubber Company, which was a cloth factory until 1886, and the Wiltshire United Dairies premises, the dye factory for it. Now there is heavy engineering, creameries and a feather purifying factory.

One of its sons, John Fowler, who was born in 1826, was the inventor of the first steam plough in 1856.

Box, known as the 'last place in Wiltshire on the road to Bath' is

Box Railway Tunnel was said to be one of Brunel's greatest designs. When constructed in 1837 it was the largest railway tunnel in the world.

mainly famous for its Tunnel. There are extensive stone quarries near here, which were used for Brunel's great works on the old Great Western Railway. The Box Tunnel, with its magnificent entrances, is said to be one of the engineer's greatest designs. When it was first constructed in 1837, its 3,212 yards in length made it the longest railway tunnel in the world. Legend says that the sun shines through it on Brunel's birthday on April 9th. At first, it was very much distrusted by travellers, many of whom refused to use it, preferring to go 'post' by horse along the road between Box and Corsham to avoid it.

Trowbridge, originally another weaver town, is now the administrative centre for the county. It was referred to in the Domesday Survey, and the town developed round the medieval castle of the De Bohuns, the curved layout of the Fore Street approximating to the line of the walls and moat.

In the 19th century, it suffered from rioting, and one of the ringleaders, Thomas Helliker, was hanged on his nineteenth birthday. He is buried in St James churchyard, his tomb lovingly subscribed by his fellow workers.

Trowbridge mills were well known and there are some delightful houses once the homes of the wool merchants. In some weavers' houses the longer upstairs windows can still be seen. They were to let in maximum light for the looms.

Today the industry is different — a brewery established in 1824, the world known Unigate dairies, and others not forgetting that firm which claims to being 'the wealth of Wiltshire' — Bowyers who make such delicious pies and sausages and bacon products.

Perhaps Trowbridge's most famous son was Sir Isaac Pitman inventor of a shorthand system who was born here in 1813. He worked in the mills counting office until he went to London at nineteen and became world known. His birthplace commemorates him with a plaque, a bust in the Town Hall and an estate, Pitman Avenue.

The poet, George Crabbe, was Rector here from 1814 to 1832 and is buried in the church.

A few miles away the delightful village of Steeple Ashton is dominated by its lovely church spire which is visible for miles. This

In the centre of Steeple Ashton the octagonal, be-knobbed lockup stands on a triangular green a market cross beside it.

place was originally another weavers' town, called Staple Ashton to mark the stone pillar in the centre of the village as a symbol of the wool market established there by Royal Charter in 1349. The name was changed to Steeple because of the church which is five hundred years old and owes much of its beauty to the generosity of the wool clothiers who paid for its construction.

The fifteenth century church is regarded as a perfect example of the Perpendicular style of fifteenth century architecture. It possesses an almost unique feature for English churches, the whole interior being designed to be vaulted in stone and the aisles were so completed, but the nave vault is of wood. There is a fine palimpsest brass to Deborah Marks who died in 1730 at the age of 99, after living under Cromwell and seven kings and queens of England. It was designed by Samuel

Edington Priory below the down was built in the fourteenth century and noble enough to be a cathedral.

Farley who produced Wiltshire's first newspaper, *The Salisbury Postman* in 1715.

The long street has old and timbered houses, and a Manor House of 1647. This is a village of charm and character, and in the centre, by the tall stone pillar, is a traditional lockup with domed roof and no windows. The village cross, beside it, dates from 1679 with a sundial on top which probably dates from 1714. The Vicarage has a fourteenth century hall and there is a half timbered post office and attractive pub.

The Priory Church of Edington is well known for its musical festivals. In 1332, William of Edington, Bishop of Winchester, but a native of the parish, founded a college for priests in the village. It became a monastery for the Augustinian Order of Bonshommes, friars of English origin who followed the rule of the Augustines at the request of the Black Prince.

Today the Priory Church is a fine example of a small monastic church of its age, and resembled a Cathedral or even a fortified mansion on account of its curious battlements. Some of its tombs were salvaged from Imber Church. There are a series of consecration crosses, with twelve inside and two on outside walls, only two missing from the complete twenty-four. No church in England has a complete set.

In the fifteenth century, this tranquil place was the scene of great violence. During Jack Cade's rebellion, William Ayscough, Bishop of Salisbury and Confessor to Henry VI, a man of some importance, was forced to escape the tumult at Salisbury. He fled to Edington taking sanctuary in the time-honoured manner. On the 29th June 1450, he was dragged from the High Altar during Mass and brutally murdered in the fields outside. His body was buried at Edington and a chapel once stood at the site of his killing.

Two centuries later, the Bemerton poet, George Herbert, married Jane Danvers in the same church.

The Priory, on the site of the original foundation is of interest, and in its garden the fishponds of the old Priory remain.

4

Castle Combe, Lacock, Corshan, Malmesbury, Chippenham, Calne and Cherhill — and a few villages

Voted 'The Prettiest Village in England', Castle Combe can be said to be something of a tourists' paradise. Of almost story-book picturesqueness, with its grey limestone cottages, complete with thatch and tiles, attractively grouped round a fifteenth century church and old market cross, it is not surprising that it was chosen for the setting for the film version of *Dr Dolittle*. It was meant to represent a fishing port and fitted the description perfectly. The old manor house, dating from the seventeenth century, is now a lovely hotel and stands a little way back from the main village. A Dower House a century younger, and the wooded hills behind (where a castle once stood giving the place its name) make an impressive background.

The river Bybrook, which runs through the village, is crossed by an old Pack Bridge (much loved by photographers) and known in 1458 as the 'great town bridge'. The Fosse Way crossed the original valley of this village which is set in a hollow and dates back to the Conquest.

It was once a weavers' village and an important market, notably for sheep at one time, with butter and eggs sold round the old market cross which is the focal point.

The Romans came here, and later there was a castle, and today it remains one of Wiltshire's undoubted showplaces. A flourishing motor track adds a touch of real modernity. Any comment would seem superfluous on this place which is a definite must for any itinerary!

And, so in natural progression, to another of Wiltshire's tourist attractions. Lacock, built on wool, which from the fourteenth to the eighteenth century, gave it prosperity, is now a property of the National Trust.

It is a beautiful example of medieval England and its early planners have left a rich heritage for any to enjoy. The narrow streets with its old cottages flanking them, only the main street in the centre wider and

Castle Combe, once a cloth-weaving centre, is a picturesque village with Cotswold stone cottages and houses, complete with stream and packhorse bridge and much beloved of tourists.

The National Trust Village of lovely Lacock, showing the lockup which consists of two rooms, one with a stone bench. Wives were said to have passed saucers of tea under the door to their husbands inside.

71

reminiscent of the days when fairs were held here and there was dancing in the open. It is another place of the unexpected, with its houses looking as fresh and natural as when they were first built. Great care is taken in their preservation, keeping modern trappings like television aerials out of sight on a nearby hill, and special lighting has been installed.

This is a 'living' village for real people, yet it possesses a friendly informality that is charming, representing every century from the thirteenth in its architecture. One building, near the shop of the National Trust, has the unusual feature of a clock let into its door.

The village was already established when Ela, widow of William Longespee, founded an Abbey for Augustinian nuns in 1232. She was the only child of the Earl of Salisbury and her father took part in the knightly coronation of Richard I. When her father died she was taken to Normandy, and a young knight, William Talbot, undertook to discover the heiress. In the guise of a pilgrim, he searched for two years and brought her back to England. She was married to William Longespee and had four sons and four daughters.

The Abbey was the last religious house to be suppressed at the Dissolution and was acquired by Sir William Sharington, and came into the possession of the Talbot family in the sixteenth century. It was here at the Abbey, that one of its famous members, William Henry Fox Talbot who served the county as Member of Parliament for Chippenham, devoted his life to photographic experiments. He made his first 'mousetrap' cameras in 1835, and in 1840 invented the first calotype and produced positive pictures from negatives. The very first photograph was the inside of a lattice window in Lacock Abbey taken in August 1835, and in 1844 his book of some twenty-four calotype illustrations taken at Lacock was produced and was the first ever photographically illustrated book. Many of his pictures were of the estate staff and one of his gamekeeper was said to be the first picture of one ever taken.

As to be expected, his name has been immortalised in the village. At the gates of Lacock Abbey a sixteenth century barn has been converted into the Fox Talbot Photographic Museum, with displays of his early photographs, letters and dark room and early equipment on display.

The Abbey itself, a feast of history with its cloisters and rooms dating back to the thirteenth century is a continuing delight to see.

The Church of St Cyriac is known for its stained glass and heraldic work and its memorials include a fifteenth century brass to a whole family, including eighteen kneeling children dated 1501.

The village is a square of streets, and has several fine old inns. The George, one of the oldest continuously licensed in England dates from 1361, and has a seventeenth century dog spit among its treasures, and

Lacock Abbey began as a nunnery in 1229, and in 1839 W.H. Fox Talbot carried out photographic experiments there.

The Sign of the Angel at Lacock is a lovely old hotel which is rich in legend.

the Sign of the Angel in another street is full of antiquity and mellow charm.

A visitor should not miss the Porch House, the lockup, rare cruck construction house of the fourteenth century and great tithe barn with eight bays.

It is a place to which people will always be drawn, and one where many locals take overseas visitors with special pride. I remember once visiting the village on a day when the Sealed Knot was re-enacting a Civil War skirmish nearby. The whole village was empty as I drove through, and then the place filled with the jingle of harness and the bustle of departure. It was like stepping back in time's pages, and I hurried on, a twentieth century intruder. I cannot help feeling that, if a medieval pagent were re-enacted today, I should feel the same in this changeless place.

Lackham House, a mile or two away, is the County's Agricultural College and was established in 1945. It also has an interesting and ever-expanding museum of farm machinery and equipment which is worth seeing.

Corsham, another village, grew into a weavers' town, though there was a settlement here in pre-Roman times. Its Flemish weavers' cottages are one of its features and there are many delightful houses to enjoy.

The churchyard has been in use for some nine hundred years, with one tomb resembling one on the field of Waterloo and another to an old lady who died in 1763 at the age of one hundred and three having grown new teeth. Truly, Sarah Jarvis was remarkable!

Other buildings to see include old almshouses, schoolroom and warden's house at the junction of the Melksham and Lacock roads. These were built and endowed by Dame Margaret Hungerford, Lady of the Manor in 1668, and have been in continuous use.

This once well known market town declined in the seventeenth century, though fairs were held from the thirteenth to the seventeenth century. The Methuen Arms Hotel has a long history and is worth a visit.

But the showpiece is, of course, Corsham Court, a royal manor in the reign of Saxon Kings, and it was on the site of the original manor house that Thomas Smythe built the present house in 1582. It was much altered in the eighteenth century by Capability Brown who tried to create an Elizabethan mansion with Georgian features!

It came into the possession of the Methuen family in 1745, when it was bought by Paul Methuen, one of the great clothiers, from his cousin, Sir Paul Methuen, who, like his father before, had been Ambassador in Lisbon and negotiated the Methuen Treaties, giving England tariff preference for Portuguese wines, and, in return, securing

The railway bridge designed by Brunel spans the line at Chippenham.

exports to Portugal of west country cloths.

Nash made changes, enlarging the house in 1800 to house further collections of the new famous Methuen pictures. Today, still the home of the Methuen family, it contains a magnificent collection of pictures and eighteenth century furniture. The Bath Academy of Art uses part of the building.

The Riding School, in the grounds, was used as a temporary church for the village when restorations to its own building were carried out from 1876 to 1878, and there are two ice houses, made in the 1760s for storing ice underground in hot weather which are still in existence today.

Corsham came into the limelight when Prince Philip served there at HMS *Royal Arthur* before his marriage to the Queen.

Chippenham, or Cippa's hamlet, was a market town in Saxon times and has close associations with Alfred the Great who lived there, hunted in the royal forest of Melksham and Chippenham, and whose sister married the King of Mercia there.

Nowadays, it is a bustling, energetic town with one of the finest cattle markets in the south of England, and a lot of industry. It is on the main line inter-city train service and near to the M4 motorway.

The Market Place forms the centre of the town with the Yelde Hall, dating from the fifteenth century, its oldest building. Once the Courts Leet and local government meetings were held there, and the borough was granted a charter by Queen Mary in 1554. A painting of arms of Elizabeth I hangs in this building which now houses the town archives.

Its medieval church is a striking one with many features of interest, including a window said to be eight hundred years old.

Chippenham is another of the county's old weaving towns and won a prize for its cloth at the Great Exhibition of 1851.

There is the River Avon flowing through it which has been known to flood on more than occasion! Among a number of old street names is one called Foghamshire derived from a stream, now known as Hardenhuish Brook, but anciently called Fokene — treacherous stream, which became corrupted to Fogham.

There are many houses of historic and architectural interest, especially those of Queen Anne and Georgian period mingling well with the older ones.

One small point of interest. The nineteenth century cheese market made the fortune of a local chemist who invented a substance, 'Anatto' to give the cheese colour and built Rowden Hill House out of the proceeds!

Many have given service to the town. One Town Clerk, F.H. Phillips, who was appointed in 1868, was, in November 1918, described as the oldest Town Clerk in England, oldest practising solicitor in Wiltshire and oldest County Court Registrar in the circuit. He continued in office until 1924 and his portrait hangs in the Yelde Hall.

But most credit for service must go to the Awdry family who are well known in the county, particularly in Chippenham. Members of this family have a continuing record of public service lasting over two hundred and fifty years, and have been seventeen times Mayors of the Borough and its Freedom was given to Colonel E.P. Awdry in 1961. This long record began in 1601 when John Awdry was Vicar of Melksham. The former Member of Parliament and one time Mayor is a direct descendant. A score card of a cricket match played in August 1872 exists between an eleven, all of whom were Awdrys against

Chippenham. The Awdrys won by an innings and three runs.

A mile or so outside Chippenham to the west is Sheldon Manor, one of the oldest houses in Wiltshire, and one of the few to have craftsmanship of the early Plantagenet times. It has been lived in for nearly seven hundred years and is still a family home. Its great porch and massive walls were built by Sir Geoffrey Gascelyn about 1282 when he held the Lordship and Hundred of Chippenham at Sheldon. The house has been added to, not least by the great Hungerford family and it is surrounded by a seventeenth century forecourt and buildings. Inside are panelled rooms with original beams, an oak staircase and much early oak furniture. It is open to the public during the year.

One of Wiltshire's most famous sons, John Aubrey, was born near Chippenham in 1626 and educated at Malmesbury and Oxford. He entered the Middle Temple, but was never called to the Bar and in 1652 he succeeded to his estate in Wiltshire.

He became immensely interested in his county and was one of the earliest topographical historians of Wiltshire being especially remembered as an antiquary and folklorist. He had many love affairs, one of which led to his temporary arrest after a lawsuit, but he did find peace in the home of Lady Long of Draycote House. On one journey from London to Draycote, he was taken ill and died at Oxford in 1697. He is probably best remembered for his *Brief Lives*, but his *Natural History of Wiltshire* makes fascinating reading.

A few miles away at Nettleton is a long, green mound with three rugged stones on top. It is one of the oldest monuments in England. The Nettleton Tumulus is in a field on the Roman Fosse Way, and, recessed into a cliff, is the site of a Roman temple to the goddess Diana which is still preserved.

In more modern times, the fourteenth century church has a rare distinction. It was struck by lightning, bearing the marks to this day, and is the only known church to have been so afflicted.

An heraldic wall monument to Samuel Arnold, a nineteenth century rector for forty years was struck in a storm in 1842.

Another of the area's prized possessions is Maud Heath's Causeway. She was a market woman who, in the reign of Henry VII, walked from Langley Burrell to Chippenham market each week to sell her butter and eggs. The path was long, muddy and dirty and she resolved to do something about it! She died in 1474 and left provision in her Will for a Causeway of stone to be built of some four and a half miles. It was raised above the ground and is carried over a series of some seventy arches, each with a span of seven feet and made of brick and stonework in-filled with flint. The grading was so skilful that the rise from the level of the lane at each end to the highest point — six feet in all — is barely perceptible. To make sure the Causeway did not fall into disrepair, she

A seventeenth century pillar was set up in memory of Maud Heath, a medieval woman whose Causeway ensures a dry walk to market.

left a considerable sum of money for its maintenance, and so it remains to this date, a memorial to a woman's determination and thoughtfulness.

Her Deed of Gift is dated 1474, and at one end she sits on a high column, basket on her arm enjoying a fine view of the county. The Causeway ends at Chippenham with a plate affixed to a stone which is inscribed.

At Langley Burrell in 1413 the young lord of the manor, Reginald de Cobham, was a follower of John Wycliffe. The teachings were held to be heretical and he was condemned to death. On the top of Steinbrook Hill he was slowly burned. Legend says that his ghost walks around the hill at midnight when the moon is full, and, somewhat surprisingly, since he was burnt, is said to carry his head under his arm!

Maud Heath's Causeway runs for four and a half miles between Chippenham and Bremhill. In 1474 she gave land to trustees which still provides money to maintain a raised footpath and bridges bearing her name.

The ancient borough of Malmesbury with its Charter dating from King Edward the Elder, claims to be the oldest in England, and its history goes back to early Saxon times. Even before then, it was a British settlement.

Famous for more than a thousand years, this market town stands high on a hill between the River Avon and its tributary, the Inglebourne, and the town, except for the northwest, is completely surrounded by water.

It owes its origin to the great Abbey which dates from the seventh century, and one of England's famous kings, Athelstan, the first to unite all the country, grandson of Alfred lies buried here. Saint Aldhelm, the

A nineteenth century statue of Maud Heath looks down on her Causeway from a neighbouring hill.

Malmesbury Abbey, a fragment of the original, whose spire, taller than that of Salisbury Cathedral collapsed in 1500, is still magnificent.

great Abbot of Malmesbury, said to have been born here, and certainly educated here, was the real founder of the Abbey and other churches including the Saxon one at Bradford-on-Avon. He was born *c.* 640 and closely related to the line of Wessex kings, dying in 709 and buried in his beloved Malmesbury. Some might say he was the first 'Salvation Army' leader in England, for, when he found people would not attend his services, he walked the town and entertained them with his harp playing and singing, then he led them back to the Abbey for service! About 700 he built the first organ in England in Malmesbury Abbey 'a mighty instrument with innumerable tones, blown with bellows and enclosed in a gilded case'.

Nowadays, a huge fragment of the abbey church stands with the Norman nave serving as the parish church, and is one of the great Norman churches of England. The nave, dated 1160, is large enough to give some idea of the size of the whole building which is enhanced by many sculptures and paintings, one reputedly by a pupil of Michelangelo. The Monks of Malmesbury wrote four immense volumes of the Bible which are among the Abbey treasures.

William the Conqueror endowed the Abbey and Edward the Confessor showered gifts upon it. The roll includes William of Malmesbury who was one of its scholars. Naturally, there is a ghost, and the ground are said to be haunted by a grey lady who disappears into a hedge.

In the fifteenth century, Malmesbury was a flourishing weaving town. One of the greatest of the clothiers was William Stumpe who was an incredible man. He was very successful, the town's Member of Parliament and became a Protestant, helping Edward VI to draft the first English Prayer Book in use until 1662.

Stumpe purchased the old Abbey from the King's Commissioners for £1,500 and restored it as the parish church, leaving much money for its preservation. At one time the Nave of the Abbey was turned into a workshop and some of the pillars bear marks to show where the looms were placed.

Apart from the Abbey, there is much to see in this town. For instance, the Market Cross dating from 1490 is one of the finest market crosses in England. Many buildings have an association with the Abbey such as the Bell Hotel next door, Stumpe's house, Abbey House, and there are other medieval inns. At Westport is a fine monastic barn, and an old well, that of St Aldhelm where the saint is said to have meditated. There is an old Court Room, a relic of the thirteenth century which is used by the Warden and Freemen of the Old Corporation.

In the past century, Malmesbury was perhaps unique in having two Corporations, the Old and the New. The former dated from 916 AD and the New came into being in 1883. Now, under the local government re-organisation, it has a Town Council, part of the North Wiltshire District.

Of its famous people possibly Oliver the Monk is most easily remembered. In 1010, he made himself a pair of wings and attempted to fly from the top of the tower of Malmesbury Abbey. He fell to the ground and was crippled for life. In 1066, on seeing Halley's Comet, he is said to have prophesied the Norman Conquest and disaster for England. One of the pubs bears his name today.

Joseph Addison, the famous writer for the *Tatler* and *Spectator*, was born at Milston near Bulford, where his father was Vicar, and was sometime Member of Parliament for Malmesbury.

Perhaps one of the saddest is a memorial in the one to a young girl, Hannah Twynnoy who, in 1703, was torn to pieces by a tiger in an exhibition of wild beasts at the White Lion Inn. Her memorial reads:
'In bloom of life she's snatched from hence
She had not room to make defence
For tyger fierce snatched life away
Until the Resurrection Day.'

The fine church and former manor of Garsdon have a strong association with the family of George Washington. It came about this way. A servant of Henry VIII gave bells to the church tower, and received the manor as a gift. He later sold it to the Washingtons. In the church is a tomb dated 1640 for Laurence Washington showing the stars and stripes which were later adopted into the design of the American flag. In this century, this tomb was restored by the Bishop of New York. Laurence Washington was cousin of the great-great-great-grandfather of the President.

Charlton Park, once the home of the daughter of William Stumpe of Malmesbury, is the seat of the Suffolk family. The twentieth Lord Suffolk, who was killed in 1941, was a very brave man. Though he was only thirty-five when he was killed, Lord Suffolk achieved much in his short life. He had been to Dartmouth, served as a Guards Officer, sailed round the world, been to Australia as a rancher and at thirty-two took his degree at Edinburgh University with first-class honours in pharmacology. At the outbreak of the Second World War, Lord Suffolk was debarred from active service by the effects of an attack of rheumatic fever and he overcame his disability by sheer determination. He did war work of a very dangerous kind, that of bomb disposal, working with a small and efficient team. For about six months he was engaged on this task then he and his team were killed together. He received a posthumous George Cross for his conspicuous bravery.

Another Lord of the Manor, the very popular television racing tipster, journalist and great jockey, Lord Oaksey lives in this area in the village that bears his name. For twenty years, John Oaksey was an amateur jockey riding under National Hunt rules. He rode in many races, including Grand Nationals coming second one year, but injury from a fall forced him to give up this sport, and he now concentrates on farming his land and his work for the *Daily* and *Sunday Telegraph* and his commentating on ITV. He also wrote a best seller on the horse, *Mill Reef*. His father, Lord Chief Justice Lawrence presided over the Nuremberg Trials at the end of the war.

Another writer who lives in the same village is Elspeth Huxley.

The village of Sherston, built partly inside an ancient earthwork, was the scene of a violent battle in 1016 when a local knight, John Rattlebone, fought the Danes. The battle was indecisive but Rattlebone, though badly wounded in the stomach, pressed a tile to his injury and fought on. He survived and was given the manor of Sherston as a reward. There is an old song in the village which goes:

Fight well, Rattlebone,
Thou shalt have Sherston.

The Church contains a huge timber chest dating from the Middle Ages, and, according to local tradition, it was used to store Rattlebone's armour. The initials 'R.B.' are carved on it.

The local inn bears a graphic picture of the Knight holding the tile to his wound and brandishing his sword.

Further south again is the town of Calne whose name is synonymous with bacon for it gained a high reputation for this product over the last two hundred years.

Formerly another weaving town, though the fine pastureland was ideal for sheep and pigs, the coming of machinery in the eighteenth century brought the decline of the wool trade.

Calne was a stopping place for travellers and the Lansdowne Arms (formerly the Catherine Wheel) is one of many old inns on the coach routes of the olden days. There was much traffic in Irish pigs from their landing at Bristol to the London markets, driving through Calne on the way. The Harris family of butchers, bought many of these pigs and Sarah Harris opened a shop in 1770. Her descendants expanded the business and the well known bacon factory was on its way. One member of the family, George Harris, went to America and returned in the middle of the nineteenth century with an idea that revolutionised bacon curing. He built an icehouse, the first factory to employ refrigeration and they took out a patent in 1864. Wiltshire ham was, like York ham, soon world known. The factory dominates the town and was granted a royal warrant in 1929.

Two of its sons gained eminence in their own fields — one was Sergeant Henry Merewether born in 1780 who became Town Clerk of London and a great municipal historian, and Attorney-general to Queen Adelaide. The other was Walter Goodall George who held the world record for the mile for thirty-seven years after achieving four minutes 12.75 seconds in 1886.

A few miles away is Bowood House, seat of the Earls of Shelburne who purchased the house in 1750. The estate was once part of the medieval forest of Chippenham and is still wooded today. When purchased, the original house was unfinished and the house has had the work of such famous architects as Keene, Adam, Dance, Cockerell, Smirke and Barry in its development. In 1955, the Big House was demolished leaving the present building as an example of eighteenth century architecture and a family house. The gardens were laid out by Capability Brown in the 1760s with magnificent spring flowers and collection of trees and shrubs. The Rhododendron Walks are famous. There is a Mausoleum designed by Robert Adam, a picture gallery and chapel which, with the gardens, are open to the public.

Dr Priestley, the celebrated chemist was librarian to Lord Shelburne (1772-79) and while working there discovered oxygen.

On the coaching route from Calne lies Cherhill, once an important staging post for travellers and one of its inns, the Black Horse, still survives.

A white horse is cut into the side of the hill. Dr Christopher Alsop, sometime Guild Steward of Calne, did so in 1780. It is 129 feet long, 142 feet high and the eye is four feet in diameter. It is said the doctor,

Bowood, seat of the Earls of Shelburne, and its estate once part of a medieval forest is still wooded.

standing a mile away from the workers, shouted instructions to them through a trumpet!

With the white horse in its shadow, the Lansdowne Monument towers majestically on Cherhill Downs and is one of the most conspicuous landmarks in the county.

The column, which rises some one hundred and twenty-five feet high, can be seen on a clear day for thirty miles. It was erected on the instructions of the Third Marquis of Lansdowne who had a passion for such edifices, in memory of his ancestor, Sir William Petty of the seventeenth century.

The contract, dated 1845, showed that Charles Barry was the designer, for which he received £92 and Daniel and Jones of Bradford-on-Avon were the actual builders at a cost of £1.359. This was a huge sum for the nineteenth century, particularly for a memorial which was later abandoned.

The Marquis had second thoughts about his ancestor, thinking it more appropriate that he should be remembered in the churchyard of Romsey Abbey where he was buried.

So this column has no inscription — only a notice to say that it is dangerous, and it became known as the Lansdowne Monument which was perhaps the original idea of its creator!

A downland place with two memorials, the White Horse cut in 1780 and the Lansdowne Monument raised in the 19th century.

The notorious Cherhill Gang, a collection of footpads, terrorised travellers in this area in the eighteenth century and were much feared. To warn them a gibbet was set up between Cherhill and Beckhampton.

One of their tricks was to strip before attacking anyone, and the sight of a naked villain in the moonlight must have been terrifying indeed. And, with the cunning of their kind, it is known that a naked man is less easily recognisable that one who appeared in the ordinary clothes of the period.

5

Devizes and its villages and the Pewsey Vale

Devizes, the old market town in the centre of the county is in the very heart of Moonraker county. It is proud of its heritage and jealous of its reputation.

It came into prominence in the eleventh century when Bishop Roger built its Castle, then said to be among the finest in Europe, and it was the scene of much turbulence especially during the wars between Matilda and Stephen. One story is that Matilda escaped from the Castle in a coffin, diguised as a corpse, which may well be true, but one fact is certain, it was she who granted the borough a charter in 1141 which was confirmed by Henry II.

Unfortunately, the Castle was destroyed by the Roundheads in the Civil War and later rebuilt in the eighteenth century as a private dwelling house. In the last War it was requisitioned as a prison for Italian prisoners of war.

The main feature of Devizes is, of course, its wide Market Place, set in a great square in the centre of the borough. There are differing, interesting buildings on all sides, and a long, long history. Weekly markets have been held since 1228 and on Thursdays since 1609, with a license for a second, on a Monday being granted in 1567, though this was discontinued in 1814. A street keeps memory alive by taking its name — Monday Market Street. A Shambles or indoor market was built in 1568 and the present, permanent building erected in 1791 with Prime Minister Addington contributing to the expense. There is a Corn Exchange which was built in 1856.

In the middle, between the parking spaces are two memorials. One is a fountain to an MP, T.H.S. Sotheron Estcourt, and a fine market cross, in memory of Viscount Sidmouth, who, as Henry Addington, was MP for Devizes and also its Recorder, Speaker of the House of Commons and Prime Minister from 1801 to 1804. (He paid for this cross himself!) Unluckily for him, it is the woman commemorated on the reverse side who is best remembered, and many think the cross is her memorial. In 1753, on the 25th January, Ruth Pierce of Potterne agreed with three other women to buy a sack of wheat in the market, each paying her portion towards the same. One of the women noticed a deficiency and asked Ruth Pierce for her contribution to make up the amount missing. Ruth protested that she had paid and said she 'wished she might drop dead if she had not'. She rashly repeated this awful wish, when, to the consternation and terror of everyone, she instantly fell down and expired, having the money concealed in her hand. Which only goes to show it does not pay to tell a lie in Devizes!

On the opposite side of the square is the Bear Hotel, an old coaching inn, made famous in the eighteenth century by the son of the landlord. For this boy was Thomas Lawrence, the portrait painter, and he began his career in Devizes, painting the travellers who visited the hotel — at the suggestion of his father. Mr Lawrence had other good ideas — one of which was to erect posts on Salisbury Plain as a guide to travellers, with S for Salisbury on one side and D for Devizes on the other. Another hotel, the Black Swan, is dated 1737, and there is an archway at the back, leading to former stables, now a market. A house bears the statue of Aesculapius on the front signifying that in 1740 it was a doctor's house.

The fine Market Place at Devizes in the heart of moonraker county where weekly markets are a feature.

The monument text reads:

The MAYOR and CORPORATION of Devizes avail themselves of the Stability of this Building, to transmit to future Times the Record of an awful Event, which occured in this Market Place, in the Year 1753, hoping that such Record may serve as a salutary Warning against the Danger of impiously invoking Divine Vengeance, or of calling on the Holy Name of GOD to conceal the Devices of Falsehood and Fraud.

On Thursday the 25th of January 1753 Ruth Pierce, of Potterne in this County agreed with three other Women to buy a Sack of Wheat in the Market, each paying her due Proportion towards the same. One of these Women in collecting the several Quotas of Money discovered a Deficiency and demanded of Ruth Pierce the Sum, which was wanting to make good the Amount. Ruth Pierce protested, that She had paid her Share and said "*She wished She might drop down dead, if She had not*" She rashly repeated this awful Wish, when, to the Consternation and Terror of the surrounding Multitude, She instantly fell down and expired, having the Money concealed in her Hand.

The Ruth Pierce Monument in Devizes Market Place commemorates a woman who told a lie there in 1753.

89

The town has its share of good houses, an Elizabethan alley of timbered ones in a busy street is where a medieval leather guild once flourished, some three hundred 'listed' buildings, among them the Queen Anne delight, Brownston House, with nearby fifteenth century Great Porch House well preserved.

The parish church of St John's, once the Church for the Castle is a major Norman church. In the twelfth century, Hubert de Burgh, the great Justician, fell foul of the King's enemies and was imprisoned in the Castle in 1233. He heard a rumour that the Bishop of Winchester was plotting his death and escaped, leaping from the walls to seek sanctuary in St John's Church. His enemies took him by force, though he 'clung desperately to the Cross'. The Bishop of Salisbury hastened to his assistance endeavouring to secure his release, but it was refused, so the captors were excommunicated. At last, he was freed, and took refuge in Wales.

Outside, in the churchyard, a strange obelisk stands, fifteen feet high, to commemorate some people who were unwise enough to go boating on a Sunday in 1751.

Beyond the Church is one of the town's prized streets, aptly named Long Street, with a collection of houses climbing to the top in a blend of Georgian and Victorian architecture. In one is the Wiltshire Archaeological Society's Museum, founded in 1853, and possessing an outstanding selection of antiquities and an excellent library.

An obelisk in St John's churchyard in Devizes, gives an awful warning to those who would go boating on a Sunday. It is in memory of some who did in 1751 and were drowned!

Fifteenth century Great Porch House in Devizes is a well preserved attraction.

There is much to see in this sturdy, independent town which has seen and overcome history, and whose earliest charter precedes that of Bristol. On the outskirts, facing the Market Place, is a huge brewery, Wadworths, from which emanates a rich, warm aroma, telling its natives that they are 'home' again — even at night — and on the road to London, the austere, modern buildings which house the Police Head-quarters remind one that Wiltshire was the first county to raise its own Force in 1839. On the other side of the road are the Le Marchant Barracks, once the home of the county's own line regiment, and still echoes to the sound of the drum on ceremonial occasions when the Wiltshire Regiment assembles in remembrance.

The Kennet and Avon Canal at Devizes has a staircase of locks that is an engineering wonder.

The Kennet and Avon Canal, which almost cuts the county in half, was the work of John Rennie, and, at Devizes, there are twenty-nine locks which rise in a spectacular staircase of engineering wonder. It is from Devizes that the well-known Canoe Race to Westminster started in 1948 and takes place annually on Good Friday. The course is some one hundred and twenty-five miles from Devizes Wharf to Westminster Bridge, and includes the negotiation of twenty-seven locks. It is described as 'one of the toughest sporting events'.

According to an eighteenth-century magazine, there was once a grave near Devizes with an ancient wooden monument with the inscription, 'A LEG IS INTERRED HERE' followed by a short poem. Alas! No trace remains now of the monument — or the leg, nor does history relate why it was buried in the first place.

Leaving Devizes in a southerly direction, the first village one finds is Potterne, driving through deep clefts cut out of the rock en route (but be wary of the warning notices permanently there against landslides!) into the sprawling village. This is an old place, its records going back to Domesday and earlier it was in the possession of the Bishops of Salisbury.

Porch House, standing on the site of an ancient hostelry, said to have been built for the Bishop of Salisbury's Steward, is a well preserved example of an early Tudor building, and known, until the beginning of this century, as Church House. For several generations, it belonged to the Pitt family, until, in 1843, it passed to Henry Oliver, High Sheriff of Wiltshire. On his death, George Richmond, the portrait painter bought it in 1870 and did much to restore it to its original beauty.

Porch House is a hall-house of the simplest plan, with a cross-gabled office part, cross-gabled chamber and solar part. During restoration in

Early Tudor Porch House at Potterne is a good example of its type and is adjoined by half-timbered cottages.

Wiltshire is known for its dewponds and this one is at Lavington.

1872, some fifteenth century French coins were found, also a mummified chicken which was thought to have been used as a foundation sacrifice. The terraced gardens have a marble well head dated 1514, which came from Venice, and, at the top of the garden, is the site of the pre-Conquest church of Potterne. The present church is thirteenth century, with a medieval pulpit and other features.

And, word of warning, don't drive too quickly out of this village, or you will miss the old hand-pump on the outskirts, and the beginning of the Plain.

There are two Lavingtons — one Market, or Lafer's Farm, which was once a flourishing market for the sale of sheep and corn until the nineteenth century. The Legend of the Drummer Boy (*Ingoldsby Legends*) originated here, and the boy is said to appear on the road across the Plain at Drummer's Post. A cottage above an old smithy belonged to Tom Smith of the 'dewponds' family. For generations, the Smiths handed down the secret of Wiltshire dewpond making, and Tom made his last in 1938, though they are still a feature of this chalky county.

West, or Bishop's Lavington is an attractive one, with a lot of history. The Church is old and interesting with a family chapel to the Dauntseys, who held the Manor, including a memorial brass to John Dauntsey, said to be the founder of the boys' school that bears his name in the village, founded in 1543.

The thatch hooks on the walls at West Lavington are a reminder of the days when thatched cottages were a fire hazard and prompt action needed to pull the thatch free.

In the graveyard is the tomb of David Saunders the 'humble, blind shepherd of Salisbury Plain' who was born in 1717 and died in 1796. He was said to have been one of Wesley's converts, and his story is told in Hannah Moore's *Shepherd of Salisbury Plain* which so interested George II that he asked for a Wiltshire shepherd to care for his flock of sheep at Windsor Castle.

Opposite a grocer's shop on a red bricked wall are two, very long, wooden hooks, once used for pulling burning thatch off roofs, and are of great length. The fireman must have been strong men, and, they have been mistaken — because of their length, for the masts of a sailing boat.

From Lavington, the great Plain stretches out, lonely and challenging, until the safety of its few villages can be reached. Today, the army is much in evidence, but long, long ago, it was a lawless place, and the old rhyme was very true:-

Salisbury Plain, Salisbury Plain
Never without a thief or twain

In 1285, a law, the Statute of Winchester, ordered that brushwood be cleared away for two hundred feet on each side of the public highway to stop robbers springing a surprise.

Some robbers tried it, and, as the memorial stone standing at Gore Cross reminds them, they were unsuccessful.

'At this spot Mr Dean of Imber was attacked and robbed by four highwaymen in the evening of October, 21, 1839. After a spirited pursuit of three hours, one of the Felons, Benjamin Colclough, fell dead on Chitterne Down. Thos. Saunders, George Waters and Richard Harris were eventually captured and were convicted at the ensuing Quarter Session at Devizes and transported for a term of fifteen years. This monument is erected by public subscription as a warning to those who presumptuously think to escape the punishment God has threatened against Thieves and Robbers.'

As if that was not enough, there is a second, similar stone, about a mile across the downs from the Tilshead to Chitterne Road, this time with quotations from the Bible to emphasise the point.

For me, one of the saddest places on the Plain is Imber which was taken over by the Army in 1943 as a training ground and gradually

A memorial stone at Gore Cross is a grim reminder of a highway robbery that failed in 1839, the year the County Police Force was raised.

A second stone was erected at Chitterne about a mile across the downs with a Biblical quotation to emphasise the moral.

demolished, with the exception of the church, which, though stripped, remains as a place of pilgrimage each September, on St Giles Day to whom it is dedicated.

A few miles away is Urchfont, the picture book village with the green and duckpond, complete with ducks, whose name is said to derive from *funta* or the spring which never runs dry.

William Pitt once owned its manor house, built in the reign of William and Mary, and the church has a tomb to Robert Tothill, Clerk of the Privy Seal to George II. One of Wiltshire's martyrs, John Bent, burnt in Devizes Market Place in 1523 for denying the doctrine of transubstantiation, was born here.

The old Salisbury coach road crosses the eastern boundaries after descending from the heights of Redhorn Hill. This is another wild, lonely stretch of the great Plain, much used by the army these days, though, when free of soldiery, makes wonderful walking country with superb views. It is possible to walk to Salisbury from here.

West of Devizes lies Poulshot, home of Wiltshire's most famous highwayman, Thomas Boulter. He was the son of a miller whose mother suffered a public whipping in Devizes Market Place, and, in 1775, he set out 'armed with the artillery of the road', to rob, and his first venture, on the road to Salisbury, was successful. He became known as the 'Flying Highwayman of Wiltshire' but when he became too easily

The picture book village of Urchfont complete with duckpond and ducks.

recognised he went north to Ripon. He was caught at York and condemned to death but reprieved on the day of execution by joining the army. For a few days he was a soldier but soon returned to his free life. At Bristol, he joined James Caldwell and this alliance was their downfall. Boulter was a reckless rogue, supper at the best places, was well dressed and was remembered at the inns he visited, and he liked to refresh his horse, said to have been another 'Black Bess' with wine. He was shot and his eye marked which led to his betrayal through the greed of an innkeeper, and this time did not escape, being executed at Winchester in 1779. He was always a popular figure, and never killed, and his ghost is still said to haunt his native village!

Izaak Walton's son was Vicar in 1688 and Bishop Ken took refuge in his vicarage when William of Orange marched on London. The pub, the Raven, is old and much connected with Boulter.

Seend is a long, straggling village, once much concerned with weaving. Henry VII encouraged some Flemish workers to settle here but they preferred Trowbridge and left, though not before adding a beautiful aisle to the church. A clothier, John Stokys, is remembered here in a fine brass and his mark — a pair of shears — is on the wall. Aubrey tried to experiment with the iron deposits found here in the hope that they might yield mineral springs like those at Bath evidently not troubling about their worth as iron ore.

To the north lie two villages with sandy soil which makes good ground for smallholdings which are common here. The hamlet of Sandy Lane was once called a thatcher's paradise for many of the cottages, the village pump, and, a rarity, the village church, are all thatched. The church was built as a private chapel in 1892 by one of the tenants on the nearby Spye Estate. There is an attractive pub, the George, where the local hunt used to meet regularly in the courtyard, and it is on the old coaching road.

Bromham, or 'Broom enclosure' a mile or two along the road, once belonged to King Harold, and is shown in Domesday as partly owned by Queen Edith, Harold's sister. (A part of the village is today called after her). In 1538, the King gave the manor to Sir Edward Baynton and the fine church has a chantry chapel in which his descendants are buried. It has much heraldry and good brasses, including one to a lady who married both a Yorkist and a Lancastrian in the Wars of the Roses!

In the distance, is Roundway Down, the scene of a fine victory for the Royalists who defeated Waller there in 1643 and dubbed it 'Runaway Down' because the enemy fled, and this battle was considered the greatest cavalry victory of the Civil War. Today, it is more peaceful and a lovely place for walks with marvellous views of the surrounding countryside.

Roundway Down the scene of a Royalist victory against Waller in 1643, and dubbed "Runaway Down" because the Roundheads fled.

The great Wansdyke with its two ends some fifty miles apart.

Bishop's Cannings Church with its majestic spire rising some one hundred and thirty feet, and a small, squat little steeple beside it.

A curious meditation chair in Bishop's Cannings Church is a dreadful chronicle of warning against wrongdoing.

To go from Devizes into the Pewsey Vale is to cross the centre of the county, and this can be a rewarding journey for there is much of interest to see on the way.

Travelling eastwards one passes the great Wansdyke (clearly marked), described as one of the 'finest linear earthworks in Britain' with the two ends of this great ditch nearly fifty miles apart, though it is no longer continuous. Its origins remain a mystery — some say it was built by the Saxons as a defence against the Danes, others that King Arthur erected it against the Saxons, though there is much evidence that it was built in the sixth century.

The first village to pause is Bishop's Cannings, said to be the setting for the Moonraker legend. It is an old, old village, the manor being a gift to the See of Sarum before Domesday and its name is really the Bishop of Sarum's Cannings, with, long gone now, a bishop's palace there.

But it has a very fine church which rises majestically on the horizon, its spire some one hundred and thirty feet high. Dating from the twelfth or thirteenth century, the church has a broad nave, wide transepts and a vaulted chancel, but perhaps its most curious possession is an old chair, sometimes called a 'Meditation Chair' which now stands in the south transept. It is a high, box-like pew, conveying its own pessimism, possibly due to the gigantic, open hand — a left one, with palm outward, which was painted to fill the surface of the upper half of the taller side of the chair. A succession of moral maxims, in Latin, are painted on the thumb, fingers, palm and wrist, in a dreadful chronicle of warning. A translation is given, but this is a sample — 'Thou shalt quickly be forgotten by thy friends — Thy heir will seldom do anything for thee — He to whom thou leavest they goods will seldom do anything for thee — Thy end is miserable.'

There has been much speculation about this strange chair, some believing it to be a pre-Reformation shriving pew, a confessional chair and a place for the monks to meditate.

James I and Queen Anne of Denmark were once entertained to music there, so it is good to know that the church organ was provided by an endowment from a local boy, William Baily, who sailed the world with Captain Cook.

There is much amusement at the small, squat little steeple which rises on the north side of the fine, tall spire, though nothing can detract from the beauty of the church itself.

The Vale, about twelve miles long, has an impressive wall of chalk hill to the south, but its northern range has the edge. The rounded hills of Martinsell, Huish, Knap Hill, Milk Hill and Tan Hill — the last with altitudes of nearly a thousand feet, tower majestically over the countryside. From Tan you can see Salisbury Cathedral spire, twenty-

Looking towards Bishop's Cannings.

five miles away, on a clear day. The countryside is fertile and some of
the best farming land in the south of England.

The villages have names which are a melody in themselves — Alton
Barnes rich in history, is best known for its White Horse, the creation of
Robert Pile, and cut in 1812. This high-stepping beast is one hundred
and eighty feet high and one hundred and sixty-five feet long, and it is
said that it cost £20, though the hired journeyman painter who agreed
to do the job is said to have vanished with the money! The church is
Anglo-Saxon, and records of village life in 1849 (*Memorials of a Quiet
Life*) by Maria Hare, wife of the Vicar recount many excitements,
including the day 'some two hundred peasants descended on the village
to break the machines on the farm'.

And here one can find Adam's Grave — not 'the' Adam — but a
Neolithic longbarrow of much antiquity which was opened in 1860.

104

Half a mile away, at Honeystreet, the Kennet and Avon canal offers a fine view from the bridge, and a tablet on the wharf recording the canal's history.

Jane Austen's sister, Cassandra, was engaged to the Vicar of Allington, and there are two unusual brasses at Alton Priors Church. The Wansdyke cuts across All Cannings where there was a British settlement dated 600BC. This was the first discovery of the Halstatt period of the early Iron Age in Britain and was made by Captain Cunnington in 1920.

In June each year an unique feast is held at Charlton to honour the memory of Stephen Duck. This local boy who became thresher and poet was honoured by Queen Caroline who became his patron, educating him and installing him as Rector of Byfleet in 1752. Unfortunately, he was much disliked by other poets and drowned himself in the River Kennet four years later. The Charlton Duck Supper, in which thirteen men drink from the Duck goblet, and the Chairman known as the Chief Duck, wears a tall hat trimmed with duck feathers, is given because the rent of a field, given in 1734 by Lord Palmerston, provides the funds.

Manningford Bruce has happy Royal associations. Mary Nicholas, sister of Jane Lane, helped Charles II to escape after the Battle of Worcester, and, in gratitude the King granted the Nicholas family the rare privilege of bearing on their arms the three lions of England. This can be seen in the memorial in the church, and the rectory is said to be haunted by the ghost of Charles, who stayed there during his escape, playing cards.

Upavon, shaped like a boomerang, is bisected by the River Avon and was once a market town. On the downs above is Casterley Camp, the largest prehistoric fortress in Wiltshire. The Central Flying School of the then Royal Flying Corps was opened here in 1912, and it became the scene of the development of night-flying techniques with many RAF instructors trained there. After the Second World War it became the headquarters of No 38 Group Transport Command.

One of Upavon's most colourful characters was undoubtedly, Henry Hunt, the farmer politician who was born at Widdington Farm in 1773. He married Miss Halcombe of the Bear in Devizes and became very prosperous, and when French invasion threatened he 'voluntarily tendered' his considerable property to the Government in case of war. Due to a misunderstanding, he received a letter from Lord Bruce saying his services in the Marlborough troop of yeomanry cavalry would be no longer required and requesting him to return his sword and pistols. Furious, he answered in person demanding satisfaction, and was fined £100 with six weeks' imprisonment. Here he met Radical politicians and later contested Bristol and Somerset. His fame as a speaker spread and he became known as 'Orator Hunt', chairing and speaking at a great assembly of eighty thousand people near Manchester when the 'Peterloo Massacre' was perpetrated in 1819. He became Member of Parliament for Preston in 1830 and died in 1835. He is remembered as 'the finest man in the House of Commons, being tall, muscular, with a healthful sun-tinged complexion and manly deportment, half-yeoman, half-sportsman'. Readiness rather than strength was characteristic of his understanding, and many of what were then considered his extreme views have since been embodied in legislation.

Pewsey, the little town of the Vale, is dominated by a statue of King Alfred in the main street, erected in 1911, and its old church has altar rails made from the timbers of the *San Josef* captured by Admiral Lord Nelson in 1797. The lock of the almsbox came from the door of a convict cell in Van Diemen's Land. The White Horse, originally cut in 1785 was re-cut in 1937 to celebrate the coronation of George VI. September is Carnival Week, and as Pewsey is known as 'the mother of West Country Carnivals', it is worth seeing.

The coronation of George V was commemorated in an unusual way in Wootton Rivers by a local man, Jack Spratt. The fourteenth century church lacked a clock until this enterprising craftsman decided to make one out of scrap metals collected by the villagers. Soon, an amazing

The crenellated toll house on the edge of Savernake Forest.

The great and mysterious Savernake Forest famed for beauty, romance and legend.

collection of old prams, pipes, bicycles and bedsteads were turned into the church clock, its castings made by a Pewsey firm. The chimes are unique, but it is the 'figures' which are the most unusual. Jack Spratt spelt out the words GLORY BE TO GOD instead of numerals.

And so on to the great forest of Savernake, famed for its beauty. The village of Great Bedwyn, on the outskirts, was the home of the Seymour family and its church has a fine brass to the brother of Queen Jane. And in the main street is an unusual museum — of Gravestones. Thomas Willis, one of the founders of the Royal Society was born here and was a friend of Christopher Wren.

Savernake Forest which belongs to the Marquis of Ailesbury, is now leased to the Forestry Commission. Famed for its beeches and great oaks, it has been a Royal Forest since the Conquest, and comprises some four thousand acres of forest with a circumference of sixteen miles. Capability Brown suggested its present layout of Avenues, yet making one whole, with each track leading to the centre. Tottenham House, once the home of the Ailesbury family, is now a boys' school, and the impressive column erected to celebrate George III's restoration to health is a fine sight.

Perhaps its most famous visitor was Henry VIII who hunted not only game but his bride in the depths of the forest. Wiltshire is proud that he married Jane Seymour of Wulfhall who became the mother of Edward VI, and her family prospered, though two of her brothers were later beheaded.

The Ailesburys are descended from Robert the Bruce and the cousin of the first Marquis fought at the famous Charge of the Light Brigade at Balaclava.

Today, the forest is a perfect place for walking, driving or picnics, and is, to me, beautiful at all times of the year.

A few miles away, at Wexcombe, one of England's farming pioneers was born. A.J. Hosier, whose family farm there still, invented a portable milk bail in the 1930s.

And for those liking machinery a visit to the Crofton Beam Engine at Great Bedwyn is high on the list. A pumping station was built in 1800 to maintain the level of the Kennet and Avon Canal water, and two early nineteenth century beam engines are to be found here. The older one, a Boulton and Watt, built in 1812 is the oldest working beam engine under steam in the world.

6

Westbury, Warminster, Longleat, Mere and the south west of the county

Defoe said Westbury was the 'chief place in the whole world for the manufacture of Spanish cloth', though Cobbett, a hundred years later, referred to it as 'a nasty, odious rotten-borough with cloth factories in it', and, indeed, it was once a well known weaving town. When the cloth trade declined, Westbury turned to another asset, iron, and the nineteenth century saw the growth of factories. Coal was also found, but not mined.

Today, most people know that Westbury has a White Horse (at nearby Bratton) the oldest in Wiltshire. It measures one hundred and eighty feet in length and is one hundred and seven feet high, with the eye alone being twenty-five feet round. It was originally cut to commemorate one of Alfred's victories over the Danes, but its outline changed at restoration in 1778.

The church possesses a chained Paraphrase of the New Testament by Erasmus and a brass to Thomas Bennet and his wife.

Nearby Dilton has one of the most attractive churches in the county. It is of fourteenth century origin, and, since Georgian times, the inside has changed little. It shows exactly how a simple, country church looked two hundred years ago with eighteenth century furnishings, plain bleached box pews, three decker pulpit and west gallery.

Bratton is also known for its Iron Age hill fort showing a complicated system of defence works covering twenty-three acres in a commanding position on the downs.

The town of Warminster dates from Saxon times and was once a royal manor. In the reign of Henry II it passed to the Hungerfords, the Howards and later the Thynnes who still retain it. At one time it was the greatest corn marketing centre in southern England as well as being another cloth town.

The Lord Weymouth School was built as a Grammar School in 1707 and Dr Thomas Arnold of Rugby fame was a pupil.

In the reign of Queen Mary, there was a quarrel between Lord Stourton, the Lord Lieutenant, and Sir John Thynne, High Steward of Warminster, which resulted in fighting. Each accused the other of treason and the quarrel ended. Four years later, Lord Stourton was hanged for a murder.

Sir Christopher Wren once tried to help the Warminster weavers by inventing a machine that would weave seven or nine pairs of stockings at once. He asked £400 for his invention, but the weavers refused to pay, saying it would spoil their trade, so he broke the model in front of them!

Outside the town, Cley Hill, a chalk height rising to some eight hundred feet, is said to be the scene of many flying saucers and other UFOs — and it does make a perfect vantage point.

The White Horse at Westbury, the oldest in the county, originally cut to commemorate Alfred's victory over the Danes.

Lord Weymouth Grammar School at Warminster where Dr Thomas Arnold was once a pupil.

Stockton, a pleasant village with a history going back many centuries is said to have the same boundaries today as in 901 when Wulfhere was lord of the manor. At one time, it was famous for its 'local customs' and Pancake Day and May Day were special celebrations. The church has monuments to three very different people — John Greenhill, who travelled the world, became Governor of the Gold Coast in the seventeenth century, and, as one of the Commissioners of the Navy laid the foundation stone of Plymouth dockyard. His ancestor, Jerome Poticary, a clothier, is commemorated in a fine brass, and there is also a small tombstone to Anne Raxworthy, a lady's maid who was so humble she asked to be buried near the porch so that everyone would 'walk over her'.

Wiltshire is ever a county of pioneers, so it is no surprise that the Marquis of Bath, whose family have owned lands in this area for generations, should be the first Peer to open his home regularly to visitors some twenty-seven years ago, thus blazing the 'Stately Home' trail.

Longleat, derived from Longa Leta, the long leat or stream, has been the home of the Thynne family for four hundred years, and was at first a monastic establishment. At the Dissolution, it passed to the Crown and in 1540 was sold for £53 to Sir John Thynne. He spent much time building, but his efforts were burnt down in 1567 and he spent a further twelve years, it is said, as his own architect, creating the house which stands today. It is a magnificent example of the Italianate style of which it remains one of the best examples of this art from Elizabeth I's reign. The Queen herself came to watch the building in progress, and the Great Hall, carefully planned by Sir John in 1559, with stone-flagged floor and hammer-beam support, remains unchanged today, except for the fireplace and Minstrels' Gallery added in 1600 and a small balcony.

The State Dining Room has witnessed much splendour and on one wall hangs a portrait of Maria Audley, first wife of Sir Thomas Thynne, third owner and grandson of the builder. She was convinced by a dream that she would die in childbirth and asked that her portrait be painted, and the dream came true.

Longleat is magnificent from any direction, but perhaps the most beautiful is to approach from Heaven's Gate, a hill-top, when all its glory lies before you. Inside there is much to see and savour — the family State Coach, built in 1750 and used at every Coronation since that of George IV in 1821. Sir Christopher Wren designed a staircase

Longleat, home of the Thynne family for over four hundred years, is one of the best examples of the Italianate style from Elizabeth I's reign. She came to watch its building.

which was removed at the suggestion of Wyatt in 1808 and — it goes without saying — Capability Brown landscaped the park.

The present Marquis, who often greets his visitors at the main door, making them as welcome as if they were indeed his personal guests, introduced another innovation, that of turning the great park into a wild-life park. Jimmy Chipperfield and his famous family joined him in the project which is now world-known, and thousands flock to see the 'Lions (and tigers) of Longleat' roaming free in natural surroundings, with others such as giraffes, rhinos, zebras and monkeys. And it is charming to see sheep grazing near the house.

It seems superfluous to say more of this wonderful place which has so much to offer any visitor.

Sir John Thynne engaged some Scottish masons when building Longleat, and, ever thoughtful for their welfare, also built them a special chapel in which to worship at Horningsham a stone's throw away. This tiny, nonconformist chapel with its thatched roof is dated 1566, and is said to be the oldest in England. The masons' cottages, called Little Scotland, still stand today.

It is fitting to go from the village and home of a Marquis to that of a Duke and see Maiden Bradley, home of the Dukes of Somerset for generations.

The name originated from the twelfth century when Henry II's

Stourhead, property of the National Trust, and loved for its gardens which are exceptional.

113

Steward founded a hospital here for 'poor women lepers', and later, when the need for a leprosy hospital had passed became a priory, long since crumbled into decay.

This village is the birthplace of Edmund Ludlow, the Parliamentarian General who was a member of the court that tried and condemned Charles I. After the Restoration of Charles II, he fled the country with other Regicides and died in exile.

The Deverills are pretty, secluded villages, and, at Longbridge Deverill, Sir John Thynne (builder of Longleat) rests in the church, his helmet on a wall.

In the eighteenth century Wiltshire was enriched by the foresight of the banking family of Hoare for they created Stourhead House in 1772. Standing in gardens which are said to be unique and outstanding in both England and Europe as an example of that period's landscape gardens, the Palladian house designed by Colen Campbell possesses a fine collection of furniture specially created for it by the younger Chippendale. Sir Richard Colt Hoare, the great patron of the arts, added wings to house his library and picture gallery.

The village of Stourton, belonged to the Stourton family for generations. In 1413 Sir William Stourton was elected Speaker of the House of Commons, and the family fortunes rose when Sir John found favour with Henry VI, becoming custodian of the Duc d'Orleans and later Treasurer of the Royal Household. He became Baron Stourton. The sixth Baron supported Henry VIII though the family were Roman Catholics, and the eighth baron was hanged for murder in the reign of Mary Tudor. Ill fortune followed in later centuries, the tenth baron being concerned in the Gunpowder Plot, and the house was sacked by the Roundheads in the Civil War.

The banker, Henry Hoare, purchased the estate in 1717 and it remained in the family for generations. A fire destroyed the central part of the house in 1902, and Sir Henry, the last baron to live at Stourhead did much to restore the building to most of its original splendour. His son died of wounds in the First World War and the house and estate was given to the National Trust in 1946, in whose care it remains, though a member of the family lives nearby.

The gardens, which were featured in the television series of *The Pallisers* are so designed that they form an entity which can be seen by a walk round the lake. Originally, the River Stour, which rises here, formed a series of ponds which were converted into a lake, on the banks of which a Grotto, the great Pantheon, completed in 1754, and a stone bridge, copied from Palladio, was built in 1762. The medieval Bristol Cross, dated 1373, was brought here from Bristol in 1765, and, with the church and village as a backcloth, makes an imposing picture.

Stourhead is an enchantment enjoyed by thousands every year, and

The Ship Inn at Mere was originally the home of Sir John Coventry who died in 1682, and who had been banished to Coventry because of remarks about his King.

another enrichment of Wiltshire's beauties.

Zeals, nudging the borders of Dorset and Somerset, stands in hilly country. Charles II hid here at the home of Colonel Grove after the Battle of Worcester, and this ancient Wiltshire family suffered, when Colonel Hugh Grove was executed in 1655 after the Penruddocke Royalist Rising in that year.

Mere is a mellow little town in the extreme south west near the source of the River Stour. The thirteenth century church, has a tower rising to one hundred and twenty-four feet. There is much to see here, particularly two brasses belonging to a former Sheriff of Hampshire — Sir John Bettesthorne, dated 1398, of whom the present Queen is a descendant, the line running from the third Duke of Buckingham to the Bowes-Lyons, the Queen being twenty-first in descent. The brass itself is unusual as it has a Dominical or Sunday letter E for the year of his death. There is a second, half brass of a man in armour, believed to be that of Sir John Berkeley, Knight and Sheriff of Wiltshire, who married Sir John's daughter.

There are two inns of particular interest. The Old Ship Hotel was

Place Farm at Tisbury was once part of the estate of the Abbess of Shaftesbury in the fifteenth century.

once the home of Sir John Coventry who was banished to Coventry in 1682 — hence the saying — and the Talbot, formerly the George, where Charles II dined after his escape following the Battle of Worcester.

The town is named after John Mere whose badge forms the basis of the wrought iron sign at the Ship Inn, and there is a connection with Margate, for both places are derived from the same Saxon name 'Mere' meaning lake or sea.

East Knoyle lies in an attractive, woodland setting in one of the loveliest parts of the county, but is especially remembered as the birthplace of Sir Christopher Wren who was born here in 1632 when his father was the rector. All trace of his home have disappeared, though there is a wall plaque to his memory.

Dr Wren worked out a plan for strapwork in his church, and lost his living in the Civil War. During his trial this scheme for strapwork was

The huge Tisbury tithe barn is said to be the second largest in England, and is more than five hundred years old and still in use.

mentioned in evidence against him in 1647. The plasterwork was eight years old then so it can be dated 1639.

The whole world knows of Sir Christopher Wren's achievements as an architect, particularly in restoring London after the Great Fire, and there are many churches to bear testimony to his skill, not least his own memorial in St Paul's Cathedral.

But he made another, perhaps greater contribution to posterity. As a young man he was keenly interested in anatomy, working with Charles II's own physician on coming down from Oxford. He began experiments for blood transfusion techniques, and, in 1656, carried out the first experiment of this kind by giving an intravenous infusion. This was a 'suspension of wine, ale, opium, scammony and other substances' which he injected into the veins of a dog to study the effects. Nine years later, this bore fruit when one of his contemporaries, Dr Richard Lower, successfully transfused blood from one dog to another.

The little village churchyard at Semley has an unusual memorial. It is of a young soldier on horseback, Lieutenant Armstrong, who was killed in 1915. His mother commissioned Henry Pegram, one of the Pegram brothers who made the Cecil Rhodes' statue in Capetown, for the memorial, the Cavell monument at Norwich. The statue, in bronze, stands about four feet high, and the officer is shown in a sun helmet and carrying a sword.

Tisbury, in wooded countryside in the sparkling Nadder Valley, is a good place to end this chapter. A small town, steeped in history, there was an abbey here in Saxon times, part of the estates of the Abbess of Shaftesbury. Place House, of the fifteenth century, belonged to her, and there is a huge tithe barn, one hundred and eighty-eight feet long, thirty-two feet wide, with thirteen buttressed bays and two porches, said to be the second largest in England. It is more than five hundred years old and is still in use.

Naturally, there is a ghost! One of the nuns at Place House was Fair Nell, a beautiful girl, who committed the sin of looking upon a man. She was condemned to walk for ever in a tunnel that (supposedly) connected the house with the top of the ridge. She is still walking.

The High Street follows the exact line of the early Saxon trackway from the Dorset coast to the Severn estuary, and, as it was built on solid rock, is almost unaltered.

The church, the largest in the area, has some Norman features though mainly dates from the seventeenth century. There is much to

Thatching the tithe barn at Tisbury.

118

A brass in Tisbury church showing a civilian and his wife *c.* 1520.

see — excellent brasses — one to an unknown civilian and his wife, dated 1520, believed to be Sir John Davies, Attorney-General for Ireland in the reign of James I whose family held lands here. But the most interesting is to Laurence Hyde his wife and their ten children, dated 1590. This man had many famous descendants — his second son was Attorney-General to Queen Anne and is buried in Salisbury Cathedral, the fourth son, Nicholas, was Lord Chief Justice, but it is the third son, Henry, who established his household at Dinton and his son, Edward, became one of England's greatest statesmen.

Edward Hyde, Earl of Clarendon, was born in 1608 and studied for the Church, later turning to the law where he was tutored by Sir Nicholas Hyde, his uncle and a brilliant scholar. In 1640 he became Member of Parliament for Wootton Bassett, and, while loyal to the King, gained the confidence of the Commons. During the Civil War, he joined the King's Party and was nominated Chancellor of the Exchequer and a member of the Privy Council, being knighted for his services. After the Battle of Naseby, he accompanied Prince Charles to Jersey where he remained for two years writing his great work, *The History of the Great Rebellion*. At the Restoration of King Charles II, he returned to England as Lord Chancellor and was made a peer, taking the title of Earl of Clarendon. He was regarded as the King's first and most confidential minister. His enemies plotted against him and an action for impeachment for high treason was started, but he fled to France where he died in 1674. His body was later buried in Westminster Abbey. His daughter, Anne, married the Duke of York, later James II, and was the mother of two Queens, Mary and Anne. At the latter's death the Hyde connection with the Royal House of Stuart ended.

A little couplet notes Clarendon's great discretion —
Lord Clarendon walks on
But naughty Samuel Pepys!

The open, sloping village of Dinton which lies in the Nadder Valley possesses an ancient British fort. However, it is the church, approached by a path arched by yew trees, that is one of the loveliest in the county. Nearly a thousand years old, the fabric dates from the twelfth century, and there were additions in the fourteenth and fifteenth centuries.

The musician, Henry Lawes, was born here in 1596. He was a celebrated composer and performer and was appointed to be one of the private musicians to King Charles I. During the Commonwealth, he supported himself by teaching music, and many poets, including Milton, admired his genius and wanted their works set to his music. He wrote the music for Milton's *Comus*. Two years before his death in 1662, he composed the anthem sung at the coronation of King Charles II.

Philipps House, designed by Sir Jeffrey Wyatville, for the Wyndham

The old Castle at Wardour once home of the Arundell family and mined to prevent the Roundheads taking it in the Civil War after a siege.

family, belongs to the National Trust, and the birthplace of Hyde and Lawes Cottage remain today.

To return to Tisbury church. There are memorials to the Arundell family of nearby Wardour Castle. One of the two Castles here is a romantic ruin and the other a school which was built for the eighth Lord Arundell in 1770.

The Manor of Wardour was held at Domesday by Sir Walter Valeran who was married to the grand-daughter of William Longespee, Earl of Salisbury. Years later, the manor passed to Sir Thomas Arundell, husband of Margaret Howard, sister of Queen Catherine, fifth wife of Henry VIII. The family were devout Catholics, and Sir Thomas was executed in 1552, his estates being restored to the family by Mary Tudor. In the reign of James I, another Sir Thomas was created Lord Arundell, and the second Baron supported the King in the Civil War raising a force at his own expense. His wife, Lady

Blanche (grand-daughter of Margaret Plantagenet, Countess of Salisbury), promised to defend the Castle if it was besieged. Though she was sixty-one years old, she resolutely held out, with only twenty-five men and servants against a Roundhead force led by Sir Edward Hungerford of over a thousand men. The siege continued and the enemy tried to attack the castle by mining it. At last, Lady Blanche was forced to obtain terms of surrender which promised quarter for all. The enemy promptly broke this treaty, plundering the valuables and sacking the castle on gaining entry. Lady Blanche, separated from her family, was sent as a prisoner to Shaftesbury, and even the clothes of the women were stolen. The enemy held the castle. Lord Arundell died of wounds received at the Battle of Lansdown, and his son, Henry, then besieged Wardour Castle. Realising it would not yield, he decided to demolish it and dislodge the Roundheads, mining his own home through underground tunnels. The enemy were dislodged, but the castle was a ruin. Lady Blanche was released and lived at Winchester, but is buried at Tisbury. Henry was later sent to prison on information by Titus Oates, but on his release was made a Knight of the Bath and a Privy Councillor. Lady Blanche's ghost still walks the castle grounds. The eighth Earl built a new castle in 1770.

The Arundell family have an American connection. The first Baron Arundell married twice, and a memorial in Tisbury church records the early days of colonisation in America, for Ann, third daughter of the second marriage, was herself married to Lord Baltimore. He petitioned the king for a charter to establish a settlement in Virginia, later amending this to an area East of the Potomac river. The new settlement was called Maryland, after Charles' Queen, Henrietta Maria. The Arundell name is still remembered in America with an Arundell County in Maryland.

Another Tisbury family has links with America. The Mayhews, established in Wiltshire in the thirteenth century, sailed to America in 1630 and, in 1641, Thomas Mayhew purchased the island of Martha's Vineyard. In Massachusetts today the Tisbury connections are not forgotten with places bearing the names of East Tisbury, West Tisbury and plain Tisbury, and Chilmark is also remembered.

In the churchyard, Rudyard Kipling's parents are buried, and there is a giant yew tree said to be a thousand years old.

7

Wilton, Amesbury, Stonehenge and some more villages

The last chapter of any book is often a sad one for the author, especially one who enjoys writing, but the south of the county, across the lovely valleys of Wylye and Woodford, through Wilton and up to Amesbury and Stonehenge, make an interesting area for description.

The country round Wardour, part of the Cranborne Chase, is much favoured for foxhunting, and the South and West Wiltshire hounds have hunted here since 1690.

The eccentric millionaire, William Beckford, born at Fonthill in 1759, was the son of a Lord Mayor of London, who derived a fortune from his West Indian estates. He was a friend of William Pitt who became god-father to his son, who, inheriting the family fortune, spent it with amazing rapidity! He built a 'Gothick dream palace' in 1796, five hundred workmen striving night and day to keep pace with the plans. Nelson and Lady Hamilton visited the site to attend a three-day and three-night party after the Battle of the Nile in 1800, before the house was complete. Beckford wanted to build a tower which would be a landmark for miles around, as high as 'St Paul's Cathedral Cross' and urged his men on to such an extent that it was constantly falling down. He moved to Bath but could still see his tower, which collapsed into ruin, taking most of his house as well. Traces of the twelve foot high wall with which he surrounded the estate still remain, and his name is remembered in the pub, *The Beckford Arms*.

A great, arched gateway to Fonthill Park, attributed to Inigo Jones, makes a splendid entrance.

Hindon is a large village, which was once planned as a town with a weekly market and annual fairs, and sent two Members to Parliament until the Reform Act of 1832. Two-thirds were destroyed by fire in 1752 and it was rebuilt in Georgian style. There is a good pub, *The Lamb*.

In World War One, Fovant was a much used army training area, and the soldiers have left a lasting memorial. They cut regimental

The Bishop's Fonthill entrance gateway which may have been the work of Inigo Jones.

badges into the chalky hillsides. No white horses for these men, many of whom came from Australia, so a map of that country, a kangaroo and a rising sun appeared on the Wiltshire landscape. An annual service is held by the badges every summer.

In addition, Fovant's church which was built in 1492, though much restored in the nineteenth century, has a most interesting brass to George Rede, its Rector in 1492, who is shown kneeling before the Annunciation in an ordinary habit. There are said to be only three examples of brasses depicting the Annunciation still surviving in England, of which this is one.

St Martin's Church at Fifield Bavant is one of the smallest churches in England, measuring thirty-five feet in length and fifteen feet in width, and it stands in a field on a grassy hill. The font is Norman and the roof beams are dark with age. Fifield is said to represent the five fields or hides of land and the Bavant comes from the Norman owners.

Compton Chamberlayne tells a brave and proud story of a man who was not afraid, and paid a terrible penalty. To visit the little church in which he worshipped and is commemorated is both a moving and uplifting experience.

Colonel John Penruddocke, our hero, was born in 1619 at his father's home, Compton House, and was educated at Blandford School, Queen's College, Oxford and Gray's Inn. In 1639, he married Arundel Freke of Melcombe in Dorset and they had seven children. He succeeded in 1648 to the estate, though the family had suffered in the Civil War as supporters of the King.

One of his ancestors, Sir George Penruddocke, distinguished himself at the Battle of St Quentin as Standard Bearer to the Earl of Pembroke, Commander in Chief of the British Army, so loyalty and service was in the blood.

John Penruddocke, disliking the rule of Cromwell, plotted with other Wiltshire conspirators, and in March 1655, they rose against the tyrant. At the head of four hundred men, Colonel Penruddocke seized the City of Salisbury, freed the prisoners, arrested the Judges and Sheriff and proclaimed Charles II King in the Market Square.

The promised Hampshire reinforcements did not arrive, so

A number of regimental badges cut into the chalk at Fovant is a lasting memorial to soldiers stationed there in World War I.

125

Penruddocke marched west, hoping to raise traditional Royalist support. At South Molton the force was attacked by Roundheads under Captain Crook from the garrison at Exeter. He promised quarter if they surrendered which they did because of overwhelming numbers. In typical Parliamentarian style, the promise was broken and Colonel Penruddocke and his friends were tried and beheaded at Exeter, though Mrs Penruddocke pleaded with Cromwell for her husband's life.

The Penruddockes' devotion both to their King and their family is moving and his final letter makes inspiring reading.

For four hundred years the Penruddocke family were connected with Compton Chamberlayne, from 1398 until October 1946 when the last of the family was buried. A tablet commemorates their deeds, the 'famous' one who fought and died to restore his rightful king and two, in later years, who gave their lives fighting in the First World War.

Once the county town of Wiltshire after which it was named — Wiltonshire — Wilton was one of the oldest boroughs in the kingdom, and said to be older indeed than the kingdom itself, of which it considered itself the parent. King Egbert's Proclamation of 838 uniting the kingdoms of Wessex and Kent was sent from 'Our Palace in Our Royal Borough of Wilton', and at that time it possessed its own mint, which closed in the reign of Henry II.

The Leprosy Queen is said to haunt a hospital of St Giles which was founded by Adelaide, second wife of Henry I, for lepers, and she has been seen within living memory — perhaps keeping an eye on her foundation. The charity still exists in the form of almshouses at Fugglestone.

In the Middle Ages, the town was under the influence of the Abbey, but, at the Dissolution, the Abbess was pensioned off to Fovant with her nuns and the estates given to Sir William Herbert, first Earl of Pembroke.

Sir William demolished the Abbey and built a fine house to which many kings and commoners came — Elizabeth I with all her court in 1573, James I (and it is claimed Shakespeare gave the first performance of *As You Like It* to please him), Charles I 'who loved it and came every summer', and soon it acquired a reputation for learning. Sir Philip Sidney wrote his book, *Utopia*, here.

Hans Holbein was the original designer of Wilton House, but much of his work was destroyed by fire in 1647, to be re-built by Inigo Jones and John Webb, and later altered by Wyatt.

Wilton House is every inch a stately home, from the Triumphal Arch surmounted by an equestrian statue of Marcus Aurelius, to the State Rooms, the Double Cube which has played its part in England's history. Originally designed by Inigo Jones and completed by Webb, it remains today exactly as it was planned. Originally a dining room, it

Wilton House, seat of the Earls of Pembroke, is one of the county's most beautiful mansions.

has been used as a drawing room and ballroom with the present Queen visiting with sovereigns from foreign countries. In the Second World War, when the house was the Headquarters of the British Army, Southern Command, this room was the 'operations room' and played its role in the planning of the invasion of France in 1944. All the paintings, with one exception, are by Van Dyck.

There is so much to see and enjoy that to describe everything would fill a book. The collections of art and antiques are among the best in England, with paintings by Rembrandt, Rubens, Van Dyck and Reynolds, Greek and Roman sculptures, Napoleon's despatch case and Queen Elizabeth I's hair. In the grounds are beautiful cedar trees of which two survive that were planted in the seventeenth century, and there is a Palladian Bridge built in 1737.

For over four hundred years, the house has been the home of the Earls of Pembroke. The Herbert family from whom they are descended, are of Welsh origin, and they came into great prominence in the reign of Henry VIII when William Herbert married Catherine Parr's sister. Before he became related to the king by marriage, William was in favour and received the Abbey and lands of Wilton.

The eighth Earl brought weavers from France, legend claims, smuggled in a cask of wine, and the carpet factory came into being, the oldest carpet factory in the world, dating from 1655, and being granted a Charter in 1699.

There have been many distinguished members of the Pembroke family who have left a rich inheritance. The Russian born Countess, mother of Sidney Herbert, Minister of War during the Crimea, was responsible for the building, by Wyatt, of the Italian style parish church.

Among Wilton's famous children are two authors, both of whom have written lovingly of their town and county. The late Edith Olivier, a native of Wilton was the daughter of a clergyman and achieved much fame through her writing. She was Wilton's first Lady Mayor in 1938, and very proud of the honour. She recalls that in the seventeenth century if the Mayor of Wilton 'stepped outside his door without his official robes, he would be fined', but, luckily, it did not apply in her time.

The second writer is Pamela Street, daughter of the farmer and writer, A.G. Street whose book, *Portrait of Wiltshire*, has become a classic in its own right.

It is not far from the tranquillity of mellow Wilton to Amesbury on the Plain, one of the oldest inhabited sites in the United Kingdom. Its name is said to derive from Ambrosius, the fifth century Roman Briton who checked the Saxon invasion. There is mention of 'Three Perpetual Choirs of Britain' which existed in pre-Saxon times, one of which is

Ambresbury, and it was claimed that in each choir were two thousand four hundred saints — a hundred for every night and day in rotation. There is testimony of a religious establishment in Amesbury, and Queen Guinevere is believed to have become Abbess after the death of the King.

The death of Guinevere was followed by what must have been one of the beautiful and tragic funeral processions ever seen. For two nights and days Sir Lancelot and his seven companions went on foot for the long, forty miles from Amesbury to Glastonbury escorting her bier, on which, her face uncovered, lay the Queen.

Malory recounts that a hundred torches were ever burning about the corpse, with Sir Lancelot and his seven fellows 'singing and reading many an holy orison, and placing frankinsense upon the body'.

If strength and poignancy of feeling are a cause of haunting, one might still meet these figures on the long, lonely road of sorrow. It is said that this beautiful vision has been seen but once, on the first tragic journey.

After the Dissolution, the property was given to Sir Edward Seymour who demolished the buildings and built a house, though he left the old Abbey church which survives as the parish church.

The Somerset family house was replaced by another Inigo Jones which was the home of the Queensberry family, and became a retreat for court authors and poets. John Gay spent much time there and it was said wrote *The Beggar's Opera* in the grounds. The Antrobus family rebuilt in 1840 and it is still known as Amesbury Abbey. In the park, beech clumps were said to indicate the positions of the English and French ships as they were at the Battle of Trafalgar in 1805.

The George Inn is said to be haunted, and there is also the Antrobus Arms which was once a school.

Years ago, Amesbury was known for its cheese, and Amesbury Abbey records show that in 1753, Truckle Cheddar type cheese were made — about nine pounds in weight.

Joseph Addison, who was born at Milston, was educated in Amesbury. It is said that the locale of shepherds and downs influenced his pen.

Once Amesbury shared a distinction with Borseley in Shropshire of making the best pipes in England. The trade waned, but specimens of the pipes, with their distinctive gauntlet marking, can still be found in museums and collections.

On a humorous note —

Invitation by a Cow

Cherry requests the pleasure of your company at Red House Farm, Amesbury, at her final milking on completion of the 365 days world's record at 12 noon on 7th April 1939. Luncheon at 12.30.

Stonehenge in all its magnificence.

This was one of the most original functions to be held in Wiltshire. This famous cow was a champion milker and 'broadcast' the whole world hearing the streams of milk which flowed into the pail when she was milked at the microphone!

Amesbury is rich in archaeological sites.

Vespasian's Camp stands on a wooded hill above the Avon, enclosing about thirty-nine acres. It is wrongly attributed to the Roman emperor for it was an English settlement long before his coming.

Casterley Camp is a hill fort whose interior contain a Belgic settlement.

Winterbourne Stoke is a compact settlement with rectangular platforms and adjacent fields.

Yarnbury Castle is another multivallate Iron Age Hill Fort.

So the road leads on to Stonehenge, described by Hardy as a 'very temple of the Winds', and by Sassoon as 'the roofless past'. Older than time itself it has stood magnificent upon the wild, brooding Wiltshire Downs for more than a thousand years before the pyramids. It is an awe-inspiring sight, approached from any angle, and even those, like myself, who have seen it many times find it an inspiration and source of wonderment.

There it stands, silent and apart, defying the ravages of man and time, and still kept its secrets. In all centuries, there have been those who have looked and wondered, yet none can claim the real truth.

LONDON
84

TO   TO
MARLBRO DEVIZES
9   5
MILES   MILES

Milestones which are a feature of some of Wiltshire's roads.

Those stones, some upright, some horizontal, have remained in their majestic circle, it seems since the world began, and yet human hand and toil were part of their creation.

The flat downland makes a marvellous background showing the monument to full advantage. They never seem diminished and in close up are fearsome in their glory.

The encircling ditch bank and holes are Neolithic and there are stone circles of sarsen stones around a horseshoe of Trilithons encompassing stones with early Bronze Age altar stones.

Stonehenge is unique. Nowhere in the world is there anything resembling its grandeur, and Wiltshiremen are rightly proud of this, their finest inheritance. It must be emphasised that they are quietly proud, they are glad it is theirs, theirs alone, and something which no one can equal. Beside it, men seem small in statue, and problems shrink. Kings and commoners alike have come to see and wonder, and it is said it is impossible to count the massive stones. Legend claims that, while staying in Wiltshire after the Battle of Worcester, Charles II stayed near here and paused to wile away the time trying to count the great stones.

The great Sarsen Circle is about one hundred feet in diameter and originally consisted of some thirty upright stones, each weighing twenty-five tons, capped by a continuous ring of thirty lintels weighing about seven tons. Inside was a pair of Sarsen Trilithons, each trilithon consisting of a pair of huge uprights, weighing up to forty-five tons, capped by a massive lintel.

Many believe as I do that Stonehenge has deep religious connections, and I am always conscious of a feeling of 'a presence' whenever I visit the place. It especially brings home the insignificance of man compared to the majesty of God. The Druid ceremonies in Midsummer seem pagan and trivial in comparison, and become a tourist attraction. Though the Druids were a Celtic priesthood, there is no evidence to sustain the belief that some stones were used for human sacrifices.

Legends abound and Geoffrey of Monmouth suggested that the stones were giants, turned to stone for a misdemeanour, condemned to stand for ever on a bleak and windy plain.

The superstitious claim that the fall of a stone is a deadly portent, and it was said that, if a lintel fell, it meant the death of a monarch. A writer in America once tried to prove that the fall of a stone foretold the deaths of Edward I and II, James II, Queen Anne, George II and IV and William IV, and the fall of one upright and one lintel of the outer sarsen circle on the last night of the nineteenth century (*The Times* 3rd January 1901) was interpreted to represent the death of Queen Victoria which occurred on the 22nd January of that year.

The stones will always attract interest. Once people believed they

The Wiltshire Downs serene in their own beauty.

held healing properties and to touch them would bring relief to sufferers, and even today, they are touched for good luck.

Everyone can put their own interpretation into Stonehenge, and surely few can remain unmoved by the majesty of the place. It gives me a sense of continuity to know that however far one wanders, one can return and find Stonehenge waiting to welcome one home. It has a quality of timelessness that gives the county its strength and puts life into new perspective, for, long after this generation is dust, Stonehenge will remain, sentinel to the winds.

After the magnificence of the original, it is fitting to turn to the Prototype of Woodhenge. This was once named a 'child's imitation of Stonehenge' and was felt to have been the wooden plan for the stone structure.

This Neolithic site, said to be one of the first major discoveries by aerial photography in Britain, was first seen by Squadron Leader Insall in 1925. Following the report of his sightings, it was investigated by archaeologists. The site is the first of a series of circular wooden structures of neolithic date to be found, and appears to be unique in this country.

It was evidently a ceremonial site for the sacrificial burial of an infant there, one of the few in England, was discovered when it was excavated.

Wiltshire is a difficult county to leave, either in writing about it or in person. For me, it will always have a fascination that goes beyond a natural affinity for one's birthplace, and I hope that others will share my pleasure at its beauties, mysteries and treasures. But, if you do not, as a Moonraker, I shall feel it will be your loss not mine.

Gazetteer

Avebury Manor, Elizabethan Manor and Gardens.

Avebury, Alexander Keiller Museum; Wiltshire Folk Life Museum and Centre, Great Barn.

Bowood House, Calne, Gardens; Picture Gallery and Chapel.

Bradford-on-Avon, Great Tithe Barn (14th century); The Halle; Saxon Church.

Broadleas House, Devizes, Gardens.

Castle Combe, village.

Chalcot House, Westbury, Palladian Manor House (17th century).

Coate Water, Near Swindon, Parkland; Leisure Centre.

Corsham Court, Elizabethan and Georgian House; Art and furniture collection.

Courts, The, Holt; Topiary; Gardens.

Crofton Pumps, Burbage, Oldest working beam engine.

Devizes, Ruth Pierce Monument, Market Place; Wiltshire Archaeological Museum, Long Street.

Great Bedwyn, Stone Masons' Museum of bygones in main street.

Great Chalfield Manor, Moated Manor House (15th century).

Kellaways, Maud Heath's Causeway.

Lackham College of Agriculture and Museum.

Lacock, Abbey (13th century Abbey and House); Fox Talbot Museum of Photography in barn; Village

Lake House

Littlecote House, Tudor Manor; Cromwellian Chapel and Armoury.

Longford Castle

Longleat, Renaissance House; Gardens; Safari Park *open all year except Christmas Day.*

Luckington Court, Queen Anne House and Gardens.

Lydiard Park, Near Swindon.

Malmesbury, Abbey.

Marshfield, Castle Farm, Working farm and agricultural museum; *Milestones* – Salisbury area in particular, Fovant Down dating back to 1756 and at Amesbury, dated 1764

Newhouse, Redlynch, Jacobean and Georgian House.

Old Sarum Castle

Phillips House,Dinton, Classical House, 1816.

Potterne, Porch House 15th century timbered house.

Pyt House, Tisbury Palladian style Georgian Mansion.

Salisbury, Cathedral; Library; The Close – Bishop's Palace, Malmesbury House (Queen Anne House), Mompesson House (Queen Anne House), North Canonry, Old Deanery *c.*1258, Wiltshire Regiment Museum, The Wardrobe, The Close; St Nicholas Hospital (thirteenth century) and South Wilts Museum; Halle of John Halle; House of John a'Port, 1425; Joiners' Hall 16th century; Old Mill, Harnham; Trinity Hospital, Almshouses.

Sheldon Manor, near Chippenham, Plantagenet Manor House.

Silbury Hill

Spye Park, Chippenham, Stables Museum.

Stonehenge

Stourhead, 18th century house and landscape gardens.

Swindon, Richard Jefferies Museum, Coate Water; Railway Museum opened 1962; Royal Wiltshire Yeomanry Museum, Bath Road.

Wardour Castle, Tisbury, Palladian House.

Wardour Castle, (Old) fourteenth century ruin.

Warminster, School of Infantry Museum.

West Kennet Longbarrow

Westwood Manor, Bradford on Avon, fifteenth century manor house; *White Horses,* see list.

Wilton, Carpet Factory (by appointment).

Wilton House, *c.*1650 House, Paintings, Gardens.

Wilton, Windmill, Near Great Bedwyn.

Archaeological Sites

All Cannings
Allington
Alton Barnes
Amesbury and nearby sites
Avebury
Bishopstrow
Cherhill
Downton (Cleobury Ring)
Enford (Chisenbury)
Fyfield and Overton
Great Bedwyn
Nettleton
Old Sarum
Silbury Hill
Stonehenge
Tisbury
Warminster
Woodhenge

Nature Trails

Marden, near Chippenham and Calne
Wansdyke, near Devizes
Savernake Forest
Brokerswood
Walker's Hill, near Pewsey
High Wood, near Westbury

Areas of natural beauty include – Cranborne Chase, Tollard Royal, Roundway Down, Salisbury Plain, Marlborough Downs, Durnford Valley, Ridgeway.

White Horses

Westbury is the oldest
Cherhill (said to be "best")
Alton Barnes, the "youngest of these three, cut in 1812
Marlborough
Pewsey

Communications

Wiltshire easily accessible by road M4, M3 and M5 in particular. Good train services to Chippenham, Swindon, Pewsey, Westbury, Salisbury. Coaches and local buses.

Tourist Information Centres

Tourist offices at Devizes, Salisbury, Marlborough, Swindon, Wilton, Trowbridge, Lacock, National Trust at Stourhead.

Lockups

There are 13 in Wiltshire, known locally as 'blindhouses', the oldest being at Bradford-on-Avon on the bridge. Many are in excellent state of preservation.

Index